EVERYBODY WINS

Everybody wins

Healthy altruism as a weapon against extreme poverty

BART COOLS
& BRUNO ROUFFAER

Children of Lima

First there almost seems to be something, there is nothing.
Only a frame.
A potential, untouched, dormant, and invisible.
Until a simple transfer of energy, call it love,
allows color to emerge from the darkness.
What transpires from it carries the DNA of many.
It ignites and awakens. Nothing becomes something.
Hands reach out, eyes look, and movement starts.
Connection becomes a fact.

Koen Vanmechelen

Foreword

In 2014, we were in Peru on a private trip and visited some development projects for potato farmers 3000 meters high in the Andes, close to Andahuaylas. We never received so many gifts as from those poor people. This came to mind when I read in Bart and Bruno's book how life satisfaction and emotional well-being do not depend on money (and yet) and that Latin America is the happiest continent.

I also begin this foreword with a positive message as in the book "Everybody wins". The subtitle is 'healthy altruism as a weapon against extreme poverty'. There have been spectacular results in all parts of the world in recent decades. Yes, there is progress! The amount of people living in extreme poverty has more than halved since the year 2000. Since 1990, over one billion people have escaped extreme poverty. Of course, as long as 10% of the world's population lives in such degrading conditions, there is still a long way to go.

Anyone who only looks at what is going wrong is missing an opportunity to give hope, the virtue that is so desperately needed today, especially in the West, consumed as it is by fear. Giving hope must, of course, be based on facts. The book offers loads of them and teaches us to read statistics carefully. The positive thinking of the two authors is not a pep talk or what the French call 'la méthode Coué', a description of autosuggestion. COVID has admittedly caused a lot of damage. Perhaps ten years of economic growth will be needed to bring the number of extremely poor back to pre-pandemic levels. There are not only the 3.8 million fatalities worldwide but some survivors have a much harder time. Inequalities were already historically high in South Africa and Latin America, but after 2020, they are even growing, also in other parts of the world. We were in the same storm, but not in the same boat.

The authors delve deeper into the question that so many have struggled with throughout history: is man good or evil? Rousseau or Hobbes? The answer recently given by a young Dutchman was: 'most people are good' (Rutger Bregman). That is also the answer of the book. Man is a survivor and he cannot do this alone. Man needs others. The cultural differences mean it is always with different emphasis and in different contexts, although these differences are much smaller than many of us think. After all, we are all human beings. Parenting plays a major role, including 'collective' upbringing based on education and leadership at all levels. If the leader spreads the poison of 'enemy thinking' it has a herd effect. Individuals easily follow the leader, especially if he warns of 'enemies'. COVID has taught us that our fates are linked. Of course, there were oblique marauders, but the vast majority followed the rules, partly out of self-preservation but also in solidarity with the most vulnerable, usually from their own families. Of course, the science of vaccines prevented us from reliving a repeat of the Spanish flu, but the authors and I are concerned with the moral aspect. In Peru, Bruno and Bart found gripping examples of solidarity. Henriette Roland-Holst already wrote a century ago: 'The soft forces will certainly win in the end', if not she said 'all warmth would freeze inside'.

There is still a lot of inhumanity today. People can become perverts if they are encouraged to do so or if there is impunity. A small group can destroy a "society". Europe has learned lessons from its tragic history and the barbaric first half of the twentieth century. This is not the case everywhere. People are sometimes blinded by being told that their nation or race is superior or that others threaten their identity. Therefore, we must be careful that we do not limit solidarity to one's tribe or family. Such tribalism is natural. Transcending the interests of one's own group requires an effort. That is where real ethics begin. No 'own poor first'!

The authors want to show how the combined efforts of people can reduce extreme poverty. It requires the right attitude of healthy altruism. I like the realism of the book. Altruism is not about saints or heroes. Giving alone is not sustainable for mere mortals. There must be room for reciprocity, for a 'return'. The vernacular says that 'love must come from both sides'. It should not be about taking or giving. It is a matter of Me and You. The Zulus and the Bantus say 'I am because you are'. That is how we become better people.

It is about searching for the meaning of life. You can never find it in the mere Ego, in the calculus towards maximum pleasure, profit or success. Meaningfulness lies in giving.

Those who live meaningful lives are most likely to find happiness. Meaning = happiness = the other.

Bruno Rouffaer and Bart Cools discovered this equation in their lives. They have "seen the light". The challenge is to live consistently from there, again not as fundamentalists and 'pure' altruists but as human beings of good will. Everybody will win.

Herman Van Rompuy
President Emeritus of the European Council
Minister of State, Belgium

Contents

INTRODUCTION   1

POVERTY

OUR VIEW OF THE WORLD IS OUTDATED   6

THE DELUSION OF RICH VERSUS POOR: DATA AS THE
ANTIDOTE   9

WALKING DOWN DOLLAR STREET   17

POVERTY IS RELATIVE   23

EXTREME POVERTY   26

VULNERABLE AREAS   34

THE DRAMATIC IMPACT OF COVID-19   39

A BROADER LOOK AT POVERTY   47

ARE WE MOVING TO BHUTAN?   52

MORE MONEY DOESN'T MEAN MORE HAPPINESS (UNLESS
YOU ARE POOR)   56

WHAT IS YOUR LENS?   63

POVERTY IN SUMMARY   67

ALTRUISM

VISIONS ON ALTRUISM   70

WHAT WE SHARE WITH OTHER SPECIES   76

INNATE OR LEARNED?   79

WE ARE SO 'WEIRD'   84

(NOT) THE PRIVILEGE OF THE RICH   88

THE ROLE OF RELIGION   91

THE SOCIAL CONTEXT   98

THE CULTURAL DIMENSION   102

PERSONAL MOTIVATIONS   110

THE UNEXPECTED EXTRAS   114

HEALTHY ALTRUISM   121

ALTRUISM IN TIMES OF COVID-19   125

ALTRUISM IN SUMMARY   129

ACTION

COMMON THINKING MISTAKES   132

THE POVERTY CYCLE   142

WHERE TO START?   145

THE HEAD AND THE HEART   151

THE WHITE SAVIOR COMPLEX   158

HEALTHY ALTRUISM IN ACTION   163

POINTS OF ATTENTION   174

OUR RESPONSIBILITY   194

ACTION IN SUMMARY   196

CONCLUSION

CASE STUDY - CHILDREN OF LIMA

THE APPEAL OF LIMA   202

THE TRIGGER   207

THE EARLY DAYS   211

AT CRUISING ALTITUDE   214

THE COVID-19 DRAMA   218

TODAY AND TOMORROW   224

CASE STUDY - TOMORROW4ISIBANI

KHETANI AND WINTERTON   230

THE SETUP AND OPERATION   232

THE AIDS PROBLEM   237

THE IMPACT OF COVID-19   240

TODAY AND TOMORROW   245

About The Authors   249
List Of Illustrations   251
Consulted Resources And Bibliography   255

INTRODUCTION

"Hi Bart, I see what you are doing, both on social media and in the field. Would love to help. Have a chat? Bruno."

A quick message between two people who had never heard of each other, sent via social media on a warm summer afternoon in Lima, Peru, received on a rainy winter evening in a small town near Brussels, Belgium. That's all it was. One of the millions of messages that crossed the Atlantic Ocean that day in a matter of seconds. The world had become very small.

Those few words triggered an exchange of WhatsApp numbers, thoughts and experiences, contacts and frustrations, good and bad news, common beliefs, and different views. When we met a year later in a bar in Antwerp, it felt like we had known each other for a long time. We had debated poverty and inequality, access to food and water, work and personal life, as well as contemporary art and wine. Not to mention our family, the constant source of energy for both of us. Four years later, those few words became the intro to a book, this book.

Extreme forms of poverty, and child poverty in particular, continue to be one of the greatest challenges of this generation. The poorest in the world often go hungry, have no easy access to education, have no light at night, and face important health problems. It is totally unacceptable that a child's future is largely determined by a twist of fate, by the place and context in which it is born. Every child comes to this earth with the same right to happiness, but enters the fray with unequal weapons.

So much for the bad news. The good news is that this doesn't need to be a fatality. In recent decades, we have made enormous progress worldwide in the fight against extreme poverty. Overwhelming proof that it can be done. However, the cards are shuffled differently for the "remaining" poor. Economic growth is less obvious in these vulnerable regions, their political situation is fragile, and the slightest conflict or natural disaster will bring them back to square one. It will take incredible political and social courage to close the "remaining" gap. But it can be done.

We are not politicians, government leaders or Nobel prize winners; we neither have the authority nor the power or knowledge to decide on such a scale. But as human beings, we have the keys and the responsibility to steer our own behavior. Every human being has a capital of altruism and decides if and how it will be used. A small decision can have a big impact on the life of a child in need. Our ambition is not to change the world, but to take action that will improve the world of a child, a family or a community. What if it was your child?

This book begins with a state-of-the-art of the poverty problem, viewed from different angles. We question several perceptions that we are often carrying with us for years. The situation today is not comparable to that two or three decades ago, both in terms of its magnitude, causes, and approach. Some areas remain extremely vulnerable, and the global pandemic has made the situation much more complex. It then describes how altruism is part of our DNA, is influenced by multiple factors, and can be activated in a variety of ways. Healthy selfishness and healthy altruism can go perfectly together, even in these COVID times. Next, we refute some common thinking errors and provide different avenues for turning our responsibility into action. Finally, we describe the path we have chosen (and how we are still making choices). We elaborate on the questions we constantly ask ourselves, the dilemmas we face, the choices we make, the lessons we have learned, and the puzzles we still haven't solved.

We have combined our own experiences with relevant data and expert research. We have not reinvented the wheel, but have taken good ideas and adapted them to the circumstances in which we work. The book is an invitation to think, understand, decide, and act. You hold the key. The choice is yours. You decide if, and in which direction, you will go. Alone, or together with others.

The book consists of chapters, each containing several topics. While it makes sense to read them in the order suggested, you can approach many of these separately. Throughout the book, we have provided links to interesting and detailed information via QR codes in case you want to explore this any further. Take what you can use, skip what you know, and enjoy what you read.

We invite you to join us on this challenging, but fascinating, instructive, and ever-enriching journey to a better world, free from extreme poverty. With healthy altruism, everybody wins: society, the receiver, and the giver.

Poverty

"In a country well governed, poverty is something to be ashamed of. In a country badly governed, wealth is something to be ashamed of."
—Confucius

OUR VIEW OF THE WORLD IS OUTDATED

What if we started this book by stating that your view of poverty is highly inaccurate? Most people have an overly negative view of the world when it comes to poverty. Figure 1 shows the results of a survey conducted in 2017 by the research firm Ipsos in 28 countries. No less than 80% of those surveyed thought that extreme poverty in the world had remained the same or even worsened over the past 20 years. However, the opposite is true: the number of people living in extreme poverty worldwide has more than halved since the start of the new millennium!

Another survey by the Dutch research bureau Motivaction, commissioned by Oxfam (conducted among 26,000 people in 24 countries and 15 languages), confirmed these findings. Here, 87% of those questioned thought that the extreme poverty situation in the world had deteriorated or remained the same. Are we all so ignorant that we collectively miss the ball?

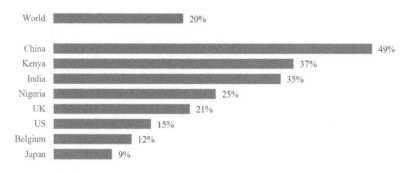

% respondents who answered that in the past 20 years
the % of the world's population living in extreme poverty has decreased

World	20%
China	49%
Kenya	37%
India	35%
Nigeria	25%
UK	21%
US	15%
Belgium	12%
Japan	9%

Figure 1: Public perceptions of the evolution of extreme poverty
(Source: Ipsos - Perils of perception. September 2017)

We see two main reasons for this distorted worldview. First, we are overexposed to information by sensationalist media. Our mental filters sift and interpret the many stimuli. The most dramatic ones win and our emotions do the rest: they blur the picture and blow things out of proportion. A picture of a starving child, no matter how horrible it is, does not mean that an entire population is affected by a life-threatening famine. Just as a crashing plane does not mean that flying would no longer be safe. Emotions cause us to see the world much worse than it really is.

Second, most of us live in countries that escaped extreme poverty several generations ago. Hence, we have not experienced the positive changes firsthand. The findings of the studies mentioned above confirm this. The proportion of correct answers differs from country to country. In countries that were low- or middle-income countries a generation ago (in 1990), people understand how global poverty has changed. They have seen the changes with their own eyes; they remember what it was like to live in extreme poverty. In China, for example, nearly 50% of those surveyed correctly stated that poverty has decreased. People in so-called rich countries do not have these reference points and therefore lack the proper perspective.

The fight against extreme poverty has been very successful over the past 20 years, regardless of what many people may believe. Unfortunately, this does not mean that extreme poverty no longer exists. It is still present in different parts of the world, sometimes very visible, often hidden. An overly negative worldview is dangerous. It is a poison that causes unnecessary anxiety and stress and leads to public pessimism where people believe that their actions to combat extreme poverty cannot make a difference. It is discouraging and does not help people find solutions or make good decisions. Instead of basing our opinions on emotions and entrenched ideas, we suggest facing reality with facts.

Ipsos
Perils of Perception
Report

Glocalities
To request the Oxfam-report
Website

THE DELUSION OF RICH VERSUS POOR: DATA AS THE ANTIDOTE

There are rich people and there are poor people, there are developed countries and there are developing countries. Either you are rich, or you are poor. That's right, or better, that was right, should you still be living in the last century!

The darker graph in Figure 2 shows the income distribution in 1975. Back then we could still speak of two separate groups: on the one hand, the poor with an income of less than $10 per person per day, and on the other hand, the rich with an income of more than $10 per day. However, the situation today, represented by the lighter graph, is completely different. The clear division seems to have disappeared.

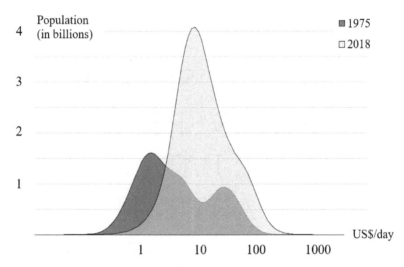

Figure 2: Comparison of global income distribution (1975 vs. 2018)
(Source: Freely available data via Gapminder.org: gapm.io/d_incm_v2)

Note: The income distribution is shown on a logarithmic X-axis to illustrate this evolution. The same distribution represented on a linear X-axis makes it clear that income inequality is still huge.

So, we can no longer divide the world into two different groups with a clear gap between them: poor countries versus rich countries, developing non-Western countries versus developed Western countries. This concept is at least 20-30 years outdated and leads to misconceptions such as "people living in Africa are poor" or "people living in the West are rich". The differences within the same country are often many times bigger than those between countries. This biased, outdated, and distorted worldview is maintained by two common errors when interpreting data: the misuse of averages and extremes.

Gapminder.org

To correct your misperceptions

Website

The (mis)use of averages

Averages are interesting and useful for measuring changes over time within a group, such as the evolution of income within a defined population group. However, they should be used with caution to avoid misinterpretations. Most data sets contain several outliers. These are data points that deviate very hard from the vast majority of other data points from the same group. For example, the CEO's salary is often many times higher than the salary of most other employees in the organization. These outliers skew the average in their direction. The high salary of the CEO in our example will lead to an average salary that is higher than what most employees earn.

A second problem with averages is that many people think of "average" as "typical," when in many groups—especially those comprising people—there are lots of exceptions to "typical." For example, a regularly misused statistic is the national unemployment rate, which is often referred to as "about x%." A closer look reveals that the average unemployment rate varies widely based on factors such as gender, age, education level, occupation, race, or geography. So, different average unemployment rates exist within the same country depending on the segmentation used. These provide a much more realistic understanding. For example, the average unemployment rate in Belgium was 7.83% in

2016, albeit with large differences between levels of education: 15.4% among those with basic and lower secondary studies, compared to 3.8% among those with higher education.

A third common error is the application of an average value to an individual case. It is a statistical error to apply the average of a group of data to a single point and assume that it is true. The probability that a data point will be equal to this average is almost the same as a random guess. Just because the average weight of a newborn boy in Belgium is 3.450 kg does not mean that every boy will weigh that much.

Using averages to compare different groups is even more dangerous. While they help simplify information, they draw our attention to the gap between two sets of numbers.

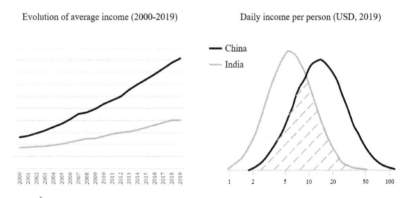

Evolution of average income (2000-2019)   Daily income per person (USD, 2019)

Figure 3: Different representations can lead to different conclusions
(illustration)
(Source: Charts based on freely available data via Gapminder.org en wid.world)

Comparing the evolution of average incomes in India and China (left-hand diagram in Figure 3) gives the impression that there is a clear divide between the two countries. In reality, the areas of overlap may be as large or even larger than the differences (right diagram in Figure 3). The same data, presented differently, can lead to very different conclusions.

The (mis)use of extremes

Besides the sometimes incorrect use of averages, we easily recall extreme examples (e.g., extremely rich versus extremely poor people) because they are more dramatic and receive more media exposure. However, such extremes are exceptions and do not reflect the majority who are in the middle. Not everyone in the United States is named Bill Gates, Elon Musk, or Warren Buffett. Just as not everyone in South Sudan is dying of starvation.

Mistakenly grouping people or countries that are very different can lead us to assume that everything or everyone in one group is equal. And, perhaps most unfortunate of all, it can make us draw conclusions about an entire category or country based on a few, or even just one, unusual example. We all know some extremely wealthy individuals from the West. However, that does not mean that every Westerner is rich. We can also easily conjure up images of extremely poor people from Africa. However, that does not mean that every African is poor.

When analyzing numbers, it is equally important to understand the differences and similarities both within and between certain groups or countries. You cannot lump everyone within a particular group or country together. So beware of hasty conclusions and generalizations and be careful with averages and extremes.

There is no longer a clearly defined gap between the West and the rest, between developed and developing, between rich and poor countries. Using this kind of terminology often wrongly suggests that there still is one, when there are more and more similarities and fewer and fewer differences.

A small exercise to illustrate. In which country are the following houses located? You will find the answers at the end of the book.

A. United States	A. Madagascar	A. South Korea
B. Kenya	B. Australia	B. Nigeria
C. The Philippines	C. Ethiopia	C. France
D. Argentina	D. Switzerland	D. Peru
E. Spain	E. Mexico	E. New Zealand

The new reality

Categorizing people as "rich" or "poor" is often wrong. Most people are somewhere in the middle where they can meet their basic needs, such as food, water, and shelter. To get a more accurate picture of how people live and how their lives change as they have more resources, we prefer to divide the world into four income levels, as described by Hans Rosling and his Gapminder organization.

People living at level 1 have to survive on less than $2 per person per day. They move barefoot to get water and eat whatever they can grow or find. A failed harvest means hunger. They cook on an open wood fire, live in shabby huts that cannot withstand extreme weather, and sleep on the ground. Due to a lack of antibiotics and accessible hospitals, illness is often a tragedy and infant mortality is high.

With an income of $2 to $8 per day, an individual is in the second tier. Their situation is less dramatic, but the slightest setback can land them in trouble. They usually have access to certain basic services such as electricity and potable water, they wear shoes or sandals and often get around by bicycle. They cook on small gas fires and can afford to purchase food regularly. They sleep on a mattress and usually have a roof over their heads. Almost half of the world's population lives at this income level.

Level 3 comprises people earning between $8 and $32 a day. Their lives are a lot more stable although often still stressful and difficult. They have tap water and can save small amounts of money with which they can buy a motor-cycle, a gas stove, or a refrigerator. They also use public transportation and eat a more varied diet. They have access to a hospital and can pay for a doctor and basic education for their children.

Finally, with an income of $32 per day, an individual belongs to level 4 or the billion richest people on earth. This group has hot and cold water, travels by car or plane, has a fully equipped kitchen, and typically goes to school for more than 12 years. They have a stable internet connection, a bathroom, insurance, and a lock on the door. All things they consider normal but which are utopian for most people at levels 1, 2, and 3.

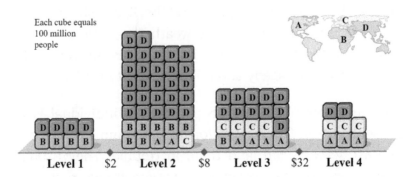

Figure 4: The world divided into four income levels (2017)
(Source: https://www.gapminder.org/fw/income-mountains/)

As shown in Figure 4, most people (5 out of 7 billion) today live at level 2 or 3, disposing of some choice and purchasing power. Although people in extreme poverty (level 1) still face high infant mortality rates, malnutrition, and terrible living conditions, they are now the minority of the world's population. Since 1990, more than 1 billion people have moved from level 1 to level 2.

Hans Rosling
About the growth of the world population
TED Talk

Our World in Data
*Research and data to make progress against
the world's largest problems*
Website

WALKING DOWN DOLLAR STREET

While the world cannot be understood without numbers, neither can it be summed up with numbers alone. Behind these numbers are real stories, real people, and real lives. If you have not experienced it yourself, it is very difficult to imagine what it is like to live with very little. Even economists who think a lot about income and poverty find it hard to understand what it means to live at such an income level.

Anna Rosling Rönnlund
See how the rest of the world lives, organized by income
TED Talk

Imagine that the world is one long street and the houses are ranked according to the income of the residents, regardless of the country they live in. This is the concept Ana Rosling Rönnlund uses in her project Dollar Street (Figure 5). Using photographs, she makes daily life tangible at different income levels in various countries. On Dollar Street, you can visit over 400 houses in 65 countries without traveling, and the list continues to grow. In each home, a photographer has spent a day taking pictures of dozens of objects, such as the family's toothbrushes or favorite pair of shoes. House numbers represent the monthly consumption values (in US dollars) available to each adult in the household. The figures consider purchasing power parity (what you can buy with a dollar in the US is not the same as what you can buy with the same amount in, say, South Africa) and are converted to US dollars.

The people and families who live on Dollar Street are real. They welcome you into their homes and are happy to show you how they live, how they cook, what they eat, how they sleep, what their toilets look like, what their children play with, and much more. A trip down Dollar Street brings the abstract concept of income levels to life. As you explore this fascinating project, you quickly realize that, on the one hand, there are great differences in living conditions between people living in the same country and, on the other hand, poverty has a similar face in different countries.

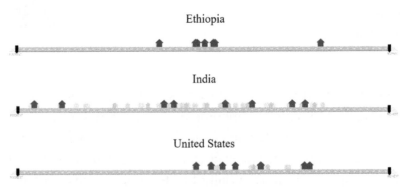

Figure 5: The Dollar Street concept
(Source: gapminder.org/dollar-street)

People can live a dozen miles from each other and yet live very far apart along Dollar Street. The Pypers and Hearne families both live in South Africa but in completely different circumstances, with monthly incomes of $90 and $3,755 respectively per adult. (Photos and text via www.gapminder.org/dollar-street).

Samantha Pypers lives with her four children and her boyfriend Rex in a slum in South Africa. Samantha is unemployed. When she lost her job, she began a relationship with a man who would later leave her with four children, the youngest of whom is disabled. The family receives help from the government. Their biggest expenses are food (70% of their income) and the maintenance of the disabled child. They eat once a day, almost always the same food, the other meals they must skip due to lack of money. They have not eaten meat for the last month, only soy, received through aid packages. The house is a construction of wood, cardboard, and corrugated iron, with a roof mostly covered with a piece of plastic. There is no electricity, no bathroom, and no toilet. They use a bucket in the bedroom and empty it into the bush afterward. Their shower and sink are also buckets. All buckets are shared with the neighbors. Tap water is available a short walk away, but it is not safe to drink it. To cook and heat the house the family uses firewood, they burn it first outside and bring it inside once it is converted to coal. The family has never been on vacation and dreams of living in a real house one day. Rex would also like to buy a used car. He estimates it will take him a year and a half to save enough money for this.

Melvina Hearne and her daughter Tshidi live in a 2-bedroom apartment in a complex secured by an electric fence. Melvina organizes school projects around culture, language, and creativity. Tshidi is in the final year of her undergraduate studies at a local university and is not yet earning an income. Electricity is used for cooking, heating, and cooling and is available without interruption. The tap water in the house is drinkable. Some household chores are done by a cleaning lady. Melvina used to live with her husband and their four children in a large house, with a swimming pool and live-in housekeepers, but after their divorce, Melvina and her four children moved to a smaller apartment, with less privacy. Meanwhile, three children have left home, and Melvina only meets them during vacations. She dreams of once again having a house large enough to accommodate all her children.

Another striking fact is that poverty has a very similar face, regardless of the country. Although the Raju and Pierro families live 15,000 kilometers apart, they are "neighbors" on Dollar Street, with a monthly income of $46 and $43 respectively per adult. Their living conditions are very similar.

Raju is 81 years old and is a rice farmer in Myanmar. He lives with his brother-in-law Myat Ang, 60, who is also a rice farmer, and his sister-in-law Lachmi, 55, who is a housewife. They live with their 3 daughters and their son Tun, 17, in a one-room house they built with the help of family and friends. They have lived there for 55 years. They like the fact that the house is close to the rice fields, but do not own the land. The house has no electricity or running water. The toilet is outside and is shared with 8 other households. The family has to buy all their food themselves, accounting for about 90% of their income. They can save almost nothing. They use wood to cook in the kitchen. They get drinking water from a nearby well. Each week, the family spends 30 hours fetching water and Lachmi spends 7 hours collecting wood and 84 hours doing housework. Their next planned investment is a car battery with which they plan to light the house. Their big dream is to one day be able to buy a piece of land.

The Pierro family lives in Haiti. Magline is 28 years old and has four children between 2 and 11 years old. She is unemployed. The family lives in a one-room house and has been there for 14 years. The house was built by family members; they do not pay rent for the building, only for the land. The house has no electricity, no toilet, and no running water. Getting water takes 2 hours a day and is not always safe to drink. The family takes care of 30% of their food needs, the remaining 70% comes from donations. Magline spends about 20 hours each week collecting firewood for cooking. Their favorite things in the house are the pots and pans. Their next purchase is a chair and their dream is to buy a house.

Gapminder.org
Dollar Street
Data

Bill Gates
Dollar Street
Video

POVERTY IS
RELATIVE

The concept of poverty is one of the first concepts our children learn in school. The teacher tells them about the "poor" children who have fewer toys, fewer clothes, and less food. They don't go on vacation and their parents don't have a car. Poor children have to take care of their little brothers and sisters. They don't watch television, they don't even have a television. They don't live in a real house either. Because poor people don't have money.

Rich and poor are explained as opposites, visually supported by graphics and photographs. A typical five-year-old child in a Western country knows the difference between rich and poor. And will probably also add that the rich children should help the poor children because that is what the teacher told them. The picture becomes more nuanced as poverty invites itself into the classroom. Kevin doesn't have a new school bag this year, his pants are worn out, he should buy a warm winter coat instead of coming to school in that light raincoat. He is now sick for the third time this year. Of course, he should wear a warmer coat. And he never invites us to his birthday party.

We soon learn that poverty exists even in our neighbor-hood. People can be poor even if they are not starving, even if they have a car and live in a house. Poverty is relative to the standard of living of the country in which the individ-ual lives. A family of four with an annual income of 15,000 dollars will be rich in one country but poor in another. They will live a decent life in Bangladesh, but in Belgium, they will have a hard time.

National poverty lines

Poverty is complex and does not mean the same thing to everyone. To measure poverty, each country defines its own poverty line, below which an individual or a family can hardly, if at all, afford to meet basic needs. The poverty line varies both over time and across countries. In most West-ern countries, this line is set at about 50% of that country's median income (i.e., the income of the person in the middle of the income distribution). Low-income countries tend to define their national poverty line by starting from the cost of a generic food requirement, such as 2,100 calories per person per day, and then adding the cost of housing, cloth-ing, electricity, and so on.

In higher-income countries, the cost of providing for one's livelihood is higher. The same is true of the poverty line. For example, where in the Democratic Republic of Congo, the national poverty line is equal to $1.40 per day, in Norway it is $35.10 per day. A Norwegian who is defined as poor can be 25 times richer than someone who is poor in the Congo, where the Gross Domestic Product per capita is 89 times lower than in Norway.

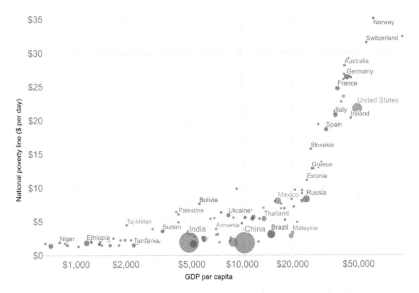

Figure 6: National poverty lines vs. GDP per capita (2016)
(Source: World Bank, Jolliffe en Prydz, via OurWorldInData.org, 2016 CC BY)

Child poverty

Using local poverty lines as a measure of relative poverty in a country also gives us a better picture of local child poverty. As Figure 7 shows, child poverty does not only exist in what we commonly call "poor" countries. In 2016, 1 in 5 children in the United States, 1 in 8 in Belgium, and 1 in 10 in the United Kingdom lived below the national poverty line.

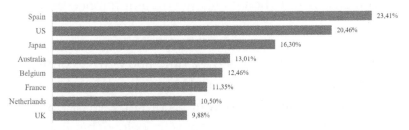

Figure 7: % of children living below the national poverty line (2016)
(Source: OECD Family database via ourworldindata.org/income-inequality)

EXTREME
POVERTY

Local poverty lines are relative to each country's income levels. They fluctuate over time and by country. They are a popular tool because they give a good indication of the proportion of a country's population that is struggling to live a decent life. Living below the local poverty line is very challenging and stressful and supporting people below the poverty line should be one of the top priorities of every government in the world.

But what if you wanted to compare poverty in different countries? Does living below the poverty line in Malawi feel the same as living below the poverty line in Belgium? To a certain extent, it probably does (life will be very difficult in both cases), but there is likely still a difference between the two.

To compare poverty levels over time and across countries, another measure is used: the International Poverty Line. This internationally agreed limit is currently set at US$1.90 per adult per day. If your income is below this line, you are living in "extreme poverty." You are most likely to be hungry and malnourished, you have limited or no access to education and other basic services, you are socially discriminated against (or excluded) and your voice does not count. You are probably not the first generation to live in extreme poverty.

As the cost-of-living increases, so does the poverty line. Since 1990, the international poverty line has increased from $1 per day to $1.25 per day, and most recently in 2015 to $1.90. This means that in 2015 it took $1.90 to buy what you could buy with $1 in 1990. In addition, this is adjusted by the World Bank for each country to consider any purchasing power differences between countries. The international poverty line thus shows the local equivalent of what you could buy with $1.90 in the United States.

Although global poverty rates have fallen by more than half since 2000, one in twelve people still live below this poverty line, and millions more live just above it. How people can survive under these economic conditions is hard for most of us to imagine. $1.90 is not even the price of a coffee in a Western country.

A few numbers:

- In 2017, 689 million people, or 9.2% of the world's population lived below the international poverty line of $1.90 per day. One in four people in the world is living on less than $3.20 a day.

- 80% of people below the poverty line live in South Asia or Sub-Saharan Africa.

· In 2018, 4 in 5 of the extremely poor lived in rural areas.

· 2 in 3 of the extremely poor are children and young people.

· About 40% of people in Sub-Saharan Africa live on less than $1.90 a day.

· In 2018, 55% of the world's population was not entitled to at least one social benefit.

· Over 40% of the world's extremely poor live in unstable countries facing conflict and violence.

· About 138 million of the world's poorest people live in high flood risk areas.

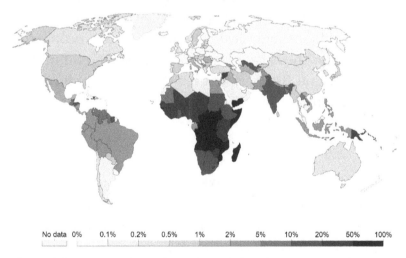

Figure 8: Proportion of population living below the international poverty line (2017)
(Source: World Bank via OurWorldInData.org/extreme-poverty/ - CC BY)

Although most of the extremely poor live in South Asia and Sub-Saharan Africa, there are still people or communities in so-called "richer" countries (such as the United States, for example) who live in a similar situation of deprivation. Homeless people living on the streets or sleeping in shelters are a vulnerable subgroup within the category of the extremely poor. While the percentages are many times lower (about 1% in the United States, less than 0.1% in Belgium and the Netherlands), behind these seemingly negligible figures are real people facing distressing situations.

Poverty and inequality

Poverty refers to people at the bottom of the income distribution, those with the lowest incomes. Inequality refers to the shape of this distribution: how large are the differences between the lowest and highest incomes? Many people feel it is inherently unfair that some people can live healthy, wealthy, happy lives while others continue to live in poor health, poverty, and grief. Unequal incomes and unequal opportunities are closely intertwined. Income poverty of one generation leads to opportunity poverty for the next generation. And less opportunity usually means less future income. The two are inextricably linked. If we want to give children equal opportunities, we must be genuinely concerned about income inequality.

Our World in Data
Global Economic Inequality
Analysis

The opportunities you have as a child depend almost entirely on where you are born. In several African countries, over one in 10 children born today will die before they are five years old. In the healthiest countries in the world—in Europe and East Asia—this will be only 1 in 250. In countries where education is most accessible—in Europe and North America—children today can count on 15 to 20 years of formal education. Children attending school in countries with the worst access to education can expect only 5 years, and of lower quality.

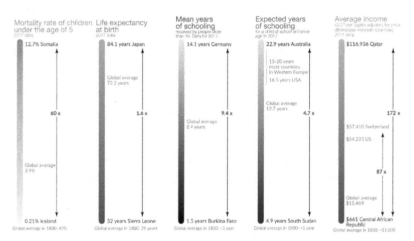

Figure 9: Inequality in living conditions (2017)
(Source: World Bank via OurWorldInData.org/global-economic-inequality CC BY)

The inequality in living conditions is so great that a person will rarely be able to close that gap by himself. His or her opportunities will only increase if the entire community and economy evolve positively. That is the essence of development and economic growth: ensuring that, what was previously only attainable by the happy few, becomes possible for most people.

Besides the differences between countries, it is important to understand the income inequality within a region or country. The gap between rich and poor is greatest in Africa and Latin America. In many countries of these regions, the top 1% of the highest earners account for 20-30% of total income, while the bottom 50% of the population only earn around 10% of total income. By comparison, in most European countries this is around 10% and 20% respectively. These figures are even more extreme when looking at wealth distribution. According to Credit Suisse's Global Wealth Report 2020, the world's 1% richest held 43% of all wealth, the poorest 50% a paltry 1%...

Credit Suisse
Global Wealth Report 2020
Report

A certain amount of inequality doesn't need to be a problem, where it encourages people to do their best, be competitive, innovate, save, and invest to get ahead in life. However, large and persistent income inequality leads to a lot of problems in society. In poorer countries, this translates into political instability, corruption, and a lack of trust in government policies that are supposed to eliminate large income disparities.

Income inequality is also a real problem in richer countries. Both Richard Wilkinson's research and a United Nations Development Program (UNDP) report show that in richer societies with high inequality, there is more mutual distrust. There are more severe punishments (partly because of stricter laws). These countries have higher stress and disease rates (because of the pressure to "watch your step") and are characterized by high rates of crime, teen pregnancy, obesity, and drug and alcohol addiction. These problems are much more common in countries such as the United States (with high income inequality) than in European countries (with relatively low income inequality).

Richard Wilkinson
How economic inequalities harm societies
TED Talk

The challenge in reducing poverty is to leave no one behind. Inequality is complex and will always exist, but with excessive inequality, social cohesion is undermined and population groups are pitted against each other. Economic growth is only healthy if the lowest incomes rise faster than the highest incomes.

The world is not on track

Substantial progress has been made in reducing extreme poverty in the last few decades. According to the most recent estimates, 8 percent of the world's population lived at or below the $1.90 a day mark in 2018. This was still 10 percent in 2015, 16 percent in 2010, and 36 percent in

1990. This means that eradicating extreme poverty should be within our grasp.

The global community made it a priority by defining "ending poverty in all its forms" as the first of the 17 Sustainable Development Goals (SDGs). These were formatted in 2015 by the United Nations as part of the new 2030 Sustainable Development Agenda. The SDGs' main reference to the fight against poverty is made in Goal 1.A: "*Ensure significant mobilization of resources from a variety of sources, including through enhanced development cooperation, in order to provide adequate and predictable means for developing countries, in particular least developed countries, to implement programs and policies to end poverty in all its dimensions.*" In summary, no one should live in extreme poverty by 2030.

Whether this will be achieved remains to be seen. The decline has slowed. Research teams from various organizations such as the World Bank, the Overseas Development Institute, the Brookings Institute, and the World Data Lab have made independent projections of the evolution of global extreme poverty through 2030. While the analyses differ in method and underlying assumptions, it is striking how aligned they are in their predictions for what we can expect over the next decade if the world maintains its current trajectory. Everyone expects a positive trend—the number of people in extreme poverty is expected to continue to decline—but everyone also agrees that the world is not on track to end extreme poverty by 2030. The number of people in extreme poverty is expected to stagnate at nearly 500 million or 5-6% of the world's population. That is terrible news.

VULNERABLE
AREAS

To put this in the right context, it is important to understand what has been the main factor behind the reduction in extreme poverty over the past two decades. Poverty decreased dramatically during that period because most of the poorest people on the planet lived in countries that have experienced strong economic growth. In Ethiopia, India, Indonesia, Ghana, and China, more than half of the population was stuck in extreme poverty a generation ago. In 1990, more than a billion of the extremely poor lived in China and India alone. Since then, those economies have grown faster than many of the world's richest countries, leading to a major reduction in global poverty. However, the situation of the remaining group of people in extreme poverty is very different.

The center of gravity of the world's poorest countries shifted in the 1990s from East Asia to South Asia and then further to Sub-Saharan Africa. Projections suggest that this geographic concentration of extreme poverty is likely to continue. If economic growth continues to follow the trajectory of the recent past, the World Bank forecasts that by 2030 about 87% of the world's poorest will live in this part of Africa.

Many of these countries have experienced very low economic growth in the past. Take the case of Madagascar: in the past 20 years, Gross Domestic Product (GDP) per capita has not grown and the number of people living in extreme poverty has increased almost proportionally to its total population. The economic engine that can lift people out of extreme poverty is sputtering or even completely missing in these countries.

Bill Gates
Living in extreme poverty
Video

Paul Collier
The "bottom billion"
TED Talk

Extreme poverty is most entrenched in so-called vulnerable areas. In these countries or regions, children and communities face higher poverty rates because of political unrest, (recent) conflicts, corrupt leaders, poor governance, gender or ethnic discrimination, and domestic violence. In addition, poor infrastructure makes access to education, clean water, health care, and other basic services very difficult. These factors not only lead to poverty but also very often impede access to social services, a crucial factor in the evolutionary process of escaping from this situation.

To end extreme poverty, these countries will have to break this vicious circle and follow the path of economic growth. This is possible, as countries like Ethiopia and India have shown, but it will require a stable context, strong governance, and strong social policies. If not, half a billion people will remain stuck with no prospect of improvement.

Such vulnerable areas still exist, on a smaller scale, in certain regions of so-called middle-income countries. This is the case, for example, in Peru, where people from the Andes migrate to Lima in search of a better life and a better future for their children. Soon they find out that they are not welcome in the capital and settle in self-built wooden shacks in the hills surrounding Lima, far away from water and electricity. Many of these newcomers have no income or savings and are left to fend for themselves. Survival becomes a daily struggle and some of them slip into extreme poverty. Over time, they organize themselves into communities. Local leaders are elected and so-called "*pueblos jóvenes*" (young villages) are born. Only when security is guaranteed, good governance practices are installed and the weakest are cared for can economic progress be made. Local stores and small soup kitchens emerge and a *wawawasi* (children's nursery) is built to care for the smallest. Siblings can go to school and parents can gradually earn a living, which quickly changes their situation. Stability, good governance, and social support create the basic conditions for economic growth that allow people to escape from extreme poverty.

The growing threat of climate change

Changing weather patterns, rising sea levels, and increased frequency and intensity of extreme weather events such as hurricanes, wildfires, and droughts are all clear indications of a rapidly changing climate. Its direct and indirect impacts present an unprecedented, additional challenge to millions of people already burdened by poverty and oppression. The struggle to earn a living, feed their families, and create a safe and stable home will become even more difficult. According to World Bank projections, depending on the scenario, between 37.6 and 100.7 million additional people will fall into extreme poverty as a result of climate change effects.

Three in four people living in extreme poverty depend on agriculture and natural resources for food and income. Changing weather patterns, drying water resources, and increasing competition for scarce resources jeopardize their available livelihoods and turn their lives and futures into an uncertain game of fortune. In addition, climate change threatens the overall food supply: floods and periods of prolonged drought make it more difficult to produce food, increasing its price, making access to it increasingly difficult, and putting the poorest families at greater risk of hunger.

In several countries such as Liberia and the Central African Republic, a large proportion of the poor lives in areas affected by both conflict and ever-increasing floods. They will have no other choice but to move, and as the situation worsens, a large influx of climate refugees will emerge, putting further strain on local economic, social, and political systems. The threats to the stability of such states and societies and the likelihood of new conflicts will only increase. In places such as Central Nigeria and Karamoja, a border region between Kenya and Uganda where resource scarcity has long been an issue, climate change has further diminished pasture and water resources, resulting in increased competition and violence.

Climate change and the tensions it creates are wiping out a good portion of the gains we have made in the fight against extreme poverty. It makes it even more difficult to close the gap and achieve the "0% extreme poverty" objective.

World Bank
Climate change in Africa will hit the poor the hardest
Video

THE DRAMATIC IMPACT OF COVID-19

Besides a sanitary catastrophe, COVID-19 unleashed a global economic disaster whose shock waves continue to spread and will be felt for a long time. The slowdown in the reduction of extreme poverty had already begun before the pandemic because of the impact of conflict, political instability, and climate change. Now, after nearly 25 years of steady decline, the numbers are increasing again for the first time, and in an unprecedented way.

Figure 10 shows the global annual evolution in the number of extremely poor from 2000 to 2020. Each bar represents the net number of people who either escaped extreme poverty or fell into extreme poverty. Over these two decades, the number of people living in extreme poverty has fallen by over 1 billion. However, the COVID-19 pandemic will nullify some of this success. It was expected that about 32 million people would escape extreme poverty in 2020, but instead of a reduction, the number will have increased by about 88 million.

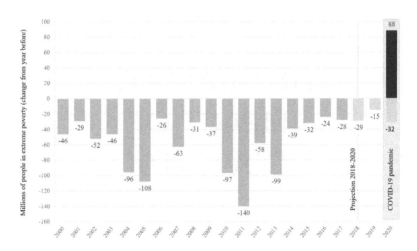

Figure 10: Annual change in the number of extremely poor (2000-2020, in millions)
(Source: Lakner et al. (2020) (updated), PovcalNet, Global Economic Prospects)

Without the pandemic, the poverty rate might have been reduced to 7.9% of the world's population in 2020; now, according to these forecasts, it will fluctuate between 9.1% and 9.4%, similar to the rate in 2017.

In addition to a group that remains stuck in poverty, many people who had escaped extreme poverty will again fall below the extreme poverty line because of the crisis. This will mainly be the case in so-called middle-income countries such as India and Nigeria. Figure 11 shows the top 5 countries where extreme poverty is likely to have increased the most in absolute terms. By far, India will feel the greatest impact. The pandemic doubly affected the country: on the one hand, much of the population was still vulnerable because they had only recently crossed the poverty line; on the other hand, economic growth was severely slowed, leaving the poorest stuck without opportunities. India had only just ceded its title of the country with the largest number of extremely poor to Nigeria but will have reclaimed that dubious honor by now.

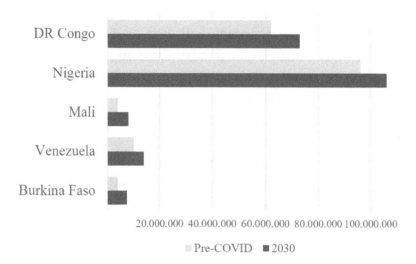

DR Congo

Nigeria

Mali

Venezuela

Burkina Faso

20.000.000 40.000.000 60.000.000 80.000.000 100.000.000

Pre-COVID ■ 2030

Figure 11: Countries with the largest likely increase in the number of people in extreme poverty due to COVID-19 (absolute numbers)
(Source: Homi Kharas, The Brookings Institute, based on IMF World Economic Outlook October 2020 and Povcal data from the World Bank)

DW News
Coronavirus pandemic puts millions at risk of poverty
Video

Temporary or permanent?

There is little doubt that 2020 will go down in the history books as an exceptionally difficult year, and it does not look like the increase in poverty rates was reversed in 2021. According to preliminary estimates, in 2021, the number of COVID-19 induced poor will have grown to between 143 and 163 million. The crisis will not be short-lived for millions of people.

Thanks to more effective infection control and the use of vaccines, the global economy will recover. The speed and strength of the recovery will vary from region to region, depending on access to medical interventions, the effectiveness of local support measures, and their structural situation before the crisis. The long-term poverty consequences will therefore be very different depending on the country in which a person lives. For most countries, COVID-19 is assumed to be a temporary shock to economic growth. The impact of the recession on poverty will be quickly reversed once economies recover. For many people who were pushed into poverty, that situation will only be temporary. This is called situational poverty, temporary poverty caused by a crisis or loss such as environmental disasters, stock market crashes, divorce, a sudden death, serious health problems, or a pandemic as we know it today. The experience of living in poverty for a relatively short period cannot be underestimated and certainly leaves its mark. Fortunately, many families have a safety net like assets they can sell, government support, or help from relatives and neighbors.

For the most vulnerable countries (those with slow economic growth), the long-term economic damage will be many times greater, with very serious consequences for families that were pushed below the poverty line. Prolonged poverty leaves lasting scars such as malnutrition, susceptibility to disease, and missed schooling. For families in poorer countries, the poverty situation could be long-term or permanent.

Figure 12 lists the countries with the largest estimated long-term poverty impact from COVID-19. Except for Venezuela and Yemen, all these countries are in Africa. Because of poor economic growth, the impact of COVID-19 could slow development for several years. For some countries with high poverty levels, such as Nigeria and the Democratic Republic of the Congo, poverty rates could even be higher in 2030 than in 2020.

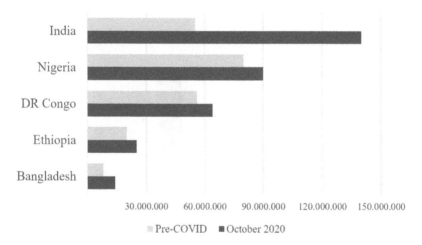

Figure 12: Estimate of the long-term impact of COVID-19 on the number of people in extreme poverty
(Source: Homi Kharas, The Brookings Institute, based on IMF World Economic Outlook October 2020 and Povcal data from the World Bank)

Magnitude of the crisis

The pandemic has triggered a global economic shock of enormous proportions. The International Monetary Fund

(IMF) estimates that the global economy has contracted by 3.5 percent in 2020—the largest global recession since World War II. By comparison, during the financial crisis in 2009, the global economy fell by just 0.1%, albeit with large differences between countries. Whereas developing countries were largely spared then and could present growth figures, this is not the case now. Figure 13 compares the economic contraction resulting from the "Great Lockdown" in 2020 with the global financial crisis in 2009.

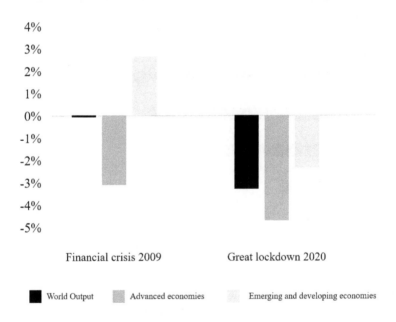

Figure 13: Economic impact of the COVID-19 crisis vs. the 2009 financial crisis
(Source: IMF DataMapper Tool, data from February 24, 2021)

The pandemic has plunged Africa into its first recession in 25 years. According to the World Bank, by the end of 2021, GDP per capita in Africa is likely to have fallen back to 2007 levels. As a result, COVID-19 could force 43 million people in Africa into extreme poverty, wiping out a minimum of five years of progress in the fight against poverty.

Rising inequality

Before the pandemic, women worldwide were already 4% more likely to live in extreme poverty than men. Now COVID-19 threatens to make this gap even wider. Women entrepreneurs have been disproportionately affected by the downsizing of economic activities because of the crisis. This is largely because women operate primarily in consumer-oriented sectors (such as services, hospitality, and retail), which were hit hardest.

In addition, the lockdowns triggered a massive digital migration. However, half of the world's population does not have access to the Internet, either through a mobile device or a fixed broadband line. Countries in Central Africa, followed by many emerging and developing economies in Asia, are among those with the lowest Internet access. For example, according to a survey by the World Bank, OECD, and Facebook, only about 60 percent of companies use email for business in Central Africa, compared to about 85 percent in Europe and Central Asia. This lack of universal and affordable Internet access increases income inequality within and between countries. Lower-income workers are less likely to work from home and are therefore not only exposed to greater health risks but also more likely to lose their jobs.

Many of the "new" poor will have a different profile than the "chronic" poor. Before the pandemic, poverty traditionally affected rural populations. Now, because of the crisis, poverty is spreading to urban areas. Sanitary measures that have brought economic activity to a standstill have left many of the poor who traditionally work in the informal economy in congested cities unable to earn a living overnight.

Finally, distance learning opportunities are very limited for the poorest children, making school dropout a real problem in some regions. UNESCO estimates that 23.8 million young people, mainly in Africa and Asia, are at risk of not returning to schools or universities after the pandemic.

The convergence of the COVID-19 pandemic with the pressures of lingering conflict and the effects of climate change is poised to completely erase years of progress in extreme poverty reduction. Instead of eradicating extreme poverty, or even reducing it to 3% of the world's population, the global poverty rate could be around 7% by 2030. According to some researchers, it will take 10 years of economic growth to reduce the number of people in extreme poverty to pre-crisis levels.

Worldpoverty.io
People in the world living in extreme poverty
Data

A BROADER LOOK
AT POVERTY

Recent World Bank estimates state that 9.2% of the world, or 689 million people, live in extreme poverty, on $1.90 or less per day. For Belgium, the poverty line in 2016 is a net monthly income of 1,115 euros for a single person or 2,341 euros for a household of two adults and two children under 14. On this basis, 15.5% of the Belgian population belongs to the group at risk of poverty.

These figures are calculated based on a person's income and ability to meet basic needs and are therefore an indication of economic poverty. To get a more nuanced understanding, it is very interesting to define poverty on different dimensions, not only based on income. Sometimes its income is above the poverty line, but a family has no electricity, no access to a decent toilet, no clean drinking water, or no one in the family has completed six years of school.

The Global Multidimensional Poverty Index (MPI) looks beyond income and considers the hardships people face in their daily lives. The index determines poverty levels in 107 low- and middle-income countries using indicators around health, education, and living standards. The index was developed in 2010 by the United Nations Development Program in collaboration with the Oxford Poverty and Human Development Initiative. According to the 2020 report, 1.3 billion people in these 107 countries are multidimensionally poor. Over two-thirds of these live in middle-income countries. Hence, the challenge of reducing multidimensional poverty is not limited to the poorest countries.

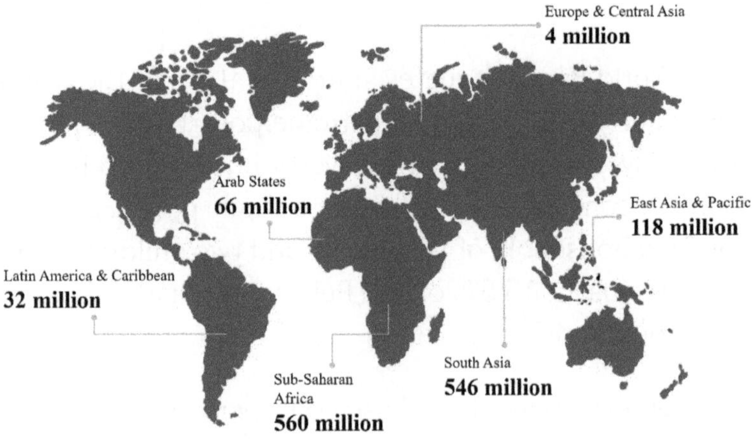

Figure 14: Number of people in multidimensional poverty by continent (2018)
(Source: hdr.undp.org/en/2018-MPI)

Within the categories of health, education, and living standards, 10 indicators are considered. If a person is deficient in one-third of these weighted indicators, he or she is considered multidimensionally poor. The MPI is calculated by multiplying the percentage of people who are multidimensionally poor (the incidence) by the average proportion of indicators in which poor people are disadvantaged (the intensity). It sheds light on the number of people living in poverty at the national and regional levels and reveals inequalities across countries and among poor people. It provides a comprehensive and in-depth picture of poverty in the world, in multiple dimensions. It is a better indicator to track progress towards the Sustainable Development Goal 1 —to end poverty in all its forms. It is also an excellent guide in determining specific interventions needed in a country to reduce and ultimately eradicate extreme poverty.

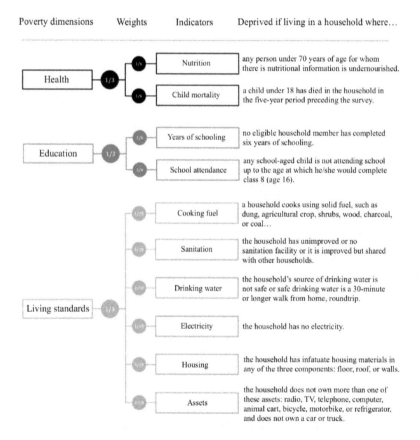

Poverty dimensions	Weights	Indicators	Deprived if living in a household where...
Health	1/3	Nutrition	any person under 70 years of age for whom there is nutritional information is undernourished.
		Child mortality	a child under 18 has died in the household in the five-year period preceding the survey.
Education	1/3	Years of schooling	no eligible household member has completed six years of schooling.
		School attendance	any school-aged child is not attending school up to the age at which he/she would complete class 8 (age 16).
Living standards	1/3	Cooking fuel	a household cooks using solid fuel, such as dung, agricultural crop, shrubs, wood, charcoal, or coal...
		Sanitation	the household has unimproved or no sanitation facility or it is improved but shared with other households.
		Drinking water	the household's source of drinking water is not safe or safe drinking water is a 30-minute or longer walk from home, roundtrip.
		Electricity	the household has no electricity.
		Housing	the household has infatuate housing materials in any of the three components: floor, roof, or walls.
		Assets	the household does not own more than one of these assets: radio, TV, telephone, computer, animal cart, bicycle, motorbike, or refrigerator, and does not own a car or truck.

Figure 15: Dimensions and indicators of multidimensional poverty
(Source: formatted based on data from ophi.org.uk)

The countries with the highest MPI values are, unsurprisingly, on the African continent: Niger, South Sudan, Chad, Burkina Faso, and Ethiopia. In absolute numbers, India is the country with the largest number of multidimensional poor, followed by Nigeria, Ethiopia, Pakistan, and Bangladesh.

United Nations Development Program
Global Multidimensional Poverty Index 2020
Report

Inequality within poverty

As mentioned earlier, totally different realities can hide behind averages, both between countries and within the same country. For example, the incidence of multidimensional poverty in Uganda is 55.1%, similar to the average in Central and Southern Africa. Thus, 55.1% of the population in Uganda lives in a situation of multidimensional poverty. But within Uganda, this figure ranges from 6.0% in the capital Kampala to 96.3% in Karamoja, the border region with Kenya. This means that in some regions of the country the percentage of multidimensionally poor households is like that of South Africa, while in other regions it is rather similar to that of South Sudan. Egypt and Paraguay have similar MPI values, but the differences in the intensity of poverty experienced by each poor person (the number of dimensions not met) are much greater in Paraguay than in Egypt. In South Asia, 10.7 percent of girls do not attend school and live in multidimensional poor households. In Afghanistan, this is 44 percent (since the Taliban seized power, this has even become close to zero). Behind every poverty is a person, a family, a situation, with its own story.

Again, children bear the greatest burden. Half of multi-dimensionally poor people are children, a third are children under the age of 10. In Burkina Faso, Chad, Ethiopia, South Sudan, and Niger, 90% or more of children are multidimensionally poor, in 30 more countries this is at least 50%.

ARE WE MOVING
TO BHUTAN?

"We don't believe in Gross National Product. Gross National Happiness is more important". So spoke the teenage king of Bhutan, the tiny state high in the Himalayas, in 1979. Since then, Gross National Happiness has become a Bhutanese philosophy. They have enshrined it in the country's constitution since 2008.

Bhutan's prime minister proposed a World Happiness Day to the United Nations in 2011, bringing international attention to happiness as an indicator. Bhutan is the only country in the world that has placed Gyalyong Gakid Palzom, or Gross National Happiness (GNH), above the Gross National Product. The philosophy is put into practice using a 30-page questionnaire that delves into the nine domains considered contributing to a person's happiness: psychological well-being, health, education, use of time, cultural diversity, good governance, community vitality, ecological diversity, and resilience and standard of living.

The list includes questions such as how often do you pray or meditate? How satisfied are you with the relationship you have with your closest relatives? How many people around you can you count on when you are sick, or when you have financial problems? And how free do you feel to express your ideas and opinions?

Since its inception ten years ago, the survey was conducted three times, the last one in 2015. During five months, 7,153 Bhutanese across the country were interviewed, and the conclusion was that GNH had grown significantly from 0.743 in 2010 to 0.756 in 2015. This would show that "people's lives are improving" and that "91.2 percent of Bhutanese were extensively or deeply happy" (GNH survey report).

The problem is that Bhutan's population at the time was 787,386, meaning that only 0.9 percent of residents were surveyed. That is a tiny sample size. It raises questions about whether GNH is a viable philosophy. According to the Bhutanese government, the philosophy acts as "a compass to a just and harmonious society". The questionnaire identifies gaps in happiness (e.g. men seem to be happier than women, and urban, educated residents are happier than rural residents) based on which they can take the necessary measures to redress the balance.

Skeptics accuse Bhutan of using Gross National Happiness as a propaganda tool to divert attention from the ethnic cleansing and human rights abuses committed by the Bhutanese government in the 1990s and to cover up the country's real problems (such as the rise of AIDS and tuberculosis, political corruption, gang violence, abuses against women, etc.).

The Himalayan kingdom is not an idyllic little country in a fairy-tale setting. It is home to 800,000 people, most of whom live in abject poverty. Their government has never denied the importance of Gross National Product, but has rearranged its position on the priority list. Gross National Happiness, they say, is a process of development and learning, rather than an objective standard or an absolute endpoint.

Whether for the right or wrong reasons, Bhutan has put happiness on the global agenda. The United Nations Sustainable Development Solutions Network released the first World Happiness Report on March 20, 2014, a date designated as the International Day of Happiness. The report ranks countries based on six key variables that support the well-being of their people: income, freedom, confidence, healthy life expectancy, social support, and generosity.

Finland is the happiest country in the world for the fourth year in a row, according to the latest World Happiness Report 2021, followed by Denmark, Switzerland, Iceland, and the Netherlands. The US ranks 19, Belgium 20, and France 21. The countries in the top 10 score high in all six variables. And that's not just about the native inhabitants of those countries. Their immigrants were also the happiest in the world. So it's not about Finnish DNA but about the way life is lived in Finland. They pay high taxes for a social safety net, they trust their government, they live in freedom and they are generous with each other. They care about each other. That's the place people want to live.

At the bottom of the list, people in Afghanistan are the least happy, followed by Zimbabwe, Rwanda, Botswana, and Lesotho. Not coincidentally, these are countries affected by extreme poverty.

And Bhutan? Bhutan did not appear on the most recent list. In 2019, it was ranked 95th.

World Happiness Report 2021
Report

MORE MONEY DOESN'T MEAN MORE HAPPINESS (UNLESS YOU ARE POOR)

Does money buy happiness? That depends on how you define happiness. How people think about their lives can differ greatly from how people live their lives. For example, if you interview two women, one with children and one without—which woman is more stressed? Usually, it's the woman with the children. But if you ask them to rate their overall life—which one is happier? Also, usually the woman with the children. This is exactly why we should measure both life satisfaction and emotions.

The 2018 edition of the annual Gallup Global State of Emotions report shows that there are regions that experience less stress and higher levels of happiness and life satisfaction than most other countries, despite the sometimes challenging or even harsh living conditions in which their populations live. So, wouldn't money be the primary key to a happy life after all? The research suggests that other elements are at least as important in the search for happiness. And this is regardless of where you live. Examples include prioritizing family, pursuing a healthy work-life balance, consciously focusing on the positive aspects of life, and a desire to make life as enjoyable as possible under all circumstances.

According to the Global Emotions Report, the happiest people live in Latin America. Latin Americans may not always rate their lives as highly as, say, people from the Scandinavian countries, but they laugh and have fun like no other people in the world. The answer to whether or not money can buy happiness is far from understood, but this report gives researchers some interesting food for thought.

Positive Experience Index – top 5	Score
Paraguay	85
Panama	85
Guatemala	84
Mexico	84
El Salvador	83

Negative Experience Index – top 5	Score
Chad	54
Niger	50
Sierra Leone	50
Iraq	49
Iran	48

Positive Experience Index – bottom 5	Score
Lithuania	51
Turkey	50
Yemen	50
Belarus	48
Afghanistan	43

Negative Experience Index – bottom 5	Score
Turkmenistan	18
Vietnam	18
Kazakhstan	17
Singapore	17
Taiwan	14

Figure 16: Positive and Negative Experience indices - highest and lowest scores (2018)
(Source: 2019 Gallup Global States of Emotions rapport)

Positive and Negative Experience Indexes

Rather than using traditional data based on economic indicators, such as Gross Domestic Product (GDP), Gallup relies on positive and negative experiences to assess the psychological state of countries or regions. Their 2019 Positive and Negative Experience Indexes measure the intangibles of life —feelings and emotions—based on over 151,000 interviews with adults conducted in 140 countries in 2018. Each index provides a real-time snapshot of people's daily experiences and offers leaders an insight into the health of their society that they cannot gather from economic metrics alone.

The Positive Experience Index is the average of all affirmative responses to a set of positive statements multiplied by 100. Country scores range from zero to 100, with higher scores indicating that positive emotions are pervasive in a country. High scores are strongly related to people's perceptions of their standard of living, personal freedoms, and social networks.

The Negative Experience Index is the average of all affirmative responses to a series of negative statements multiplied by 100. Again, the country scores range from zero to 100. The higher the score, the more pronounced negative emotions are in a country. Health problems and lack of access to food are typically good predictors of higher negative scores.

Gallup
Global Emotions Report 2019
Report

Americans are more stressed

55% of Americans reported being stressed for much of the day. That's the highest score of any country except for Greece (at 59% the world's number one stress country as of 2012, more than 20% above the global average), the Philippines, and Tanzania.

In addition, nearly half of Americans felt worried (45%) and more than a fifth (22%) felt angry, an increase over 2017. Despite strong economic results, more Americans were stressed, angry, and worried in 2018 than in the past decade, a situation that has only worsened during President Trump's tenure.

The saddest country

Americans were more stressed than the people of Chad, the world's saddest population. 51% of Chadians reported being stressed in 2017, 54% reported sadness, and 66% felt anxious and felt physical pain. The country suffers from inadequate infrastructure and is torn by internal conflict, while health and social conditions are unfavorable compared to other countries in the region.

According to Gallup, the country's overall score reflects the violence, displacement, and collapse of basic services that have affected thousands of families in large parts of Chad. Seven in 10 residents struggled to afford food that year. The West African countries of Niger and Sierra Leone are number 2 and 3 in Gallup's report. Iraq and Iran complete the top five.

Latin American countries are the most positive. But why?

A raft of Latin American countries leads the way on the most positive list. Guatemala, Mexico, and El Salvador follow in the wake of Paraguay and Panama. The top 10 of the most positive countries is entirely Latin American, except for Indonesia. And this is no coincidence; Latin American countries top the list year after year. The scores seem to be related to strong social networks and a good balance between family and work. Most Latin Americans are so strongly focused on their families that it seems to give them a sense of "no matter what, I always have you". This family focus, for example, is an integral part of everyday culture in Paraguay. Paraguayans usually work from 7 to 11 a.m., before going home to have lunch and relax with their families. They resume work from 3 to 7 in the evening, which is very different from most other countries.

These figures predate the COVID-19 outbreak. Many of the people interviewed by Gallup entered the crisis with a state of mind that was already negative, which may not bode well for their situation during or after the pandemic.

Money and happiness

People in richer countries are more satisfied with their lives than people in poorer countries. Also, within the same country, richer people are happier than poorer people. However, the relationship between income and happiness is not linear: at a low income, a small increase might have a large impact on your sense of happiness. At a high income, even a notable increase will have only a small impact on one's happiness. From a certain point, more money does not make you happier.

One of the most important studies on the link between money and happiness was conducted in 2010 by the later Nobel prize winners, Daniel Kahneman and Angus Deaton. They found that the more money Americans made, the higher they rated their lives. So, if happiness is how people view their lives, then money makes people happier. This is also true internationally. The World Happiness Report shows that the richer the country, the higher people rate their lives (see Figure 17). Although there are exceptions to this statement, such as Uzbeks who seem to be happier than Hong Kong residents, even though their income is ten times lower on average.

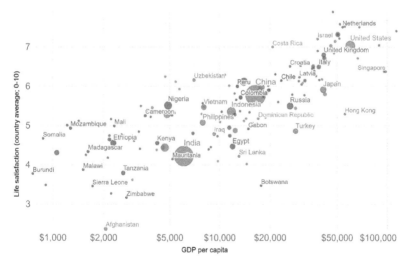

Figure 17: Self-reported life satisfaction vs. GDP per capita (2017)
(Source: World Happiness Report (2019), via OurWorldInData.org/ happiness-and-life-satisfaction/)

But how does money affect the way people live? The Kahneman and Deaton study found that starting at an income of $75,000, money has less influence on how people live their lives. Their findings were confirmed in a 2018 study at Purdue University and the University of Virginia that showed that there seems to be a saturation point—around $100,000 a year—and that being too rich can even make your life a little less pleasant. According to the researchers, the optimum for emotional well-being would be about $60,000 to $75,000. They analyzed variables such as pleasure, smiles and laughter, tranquility, feelings of respect, and intellectual stimulation, as well as negative emotions such as anger, stress, sadness, physical pain, and worry.

Concluding that money is not important and that people living in extreme poverty could also be perfectly happy is a bridge too far. More money does not necessarily make one happier, not enough money, usually makes one unhappy. Living on a very low income is not romantic at all.

WHAT IS YOUR LENS?

Through the lens of someone living in a "rich" country, the perception of life for people living in extreme poverty is usually distorted. Low-income countries are much more developed than most people think. And far fewer people live there than most of us think. Conversely, some high-income countries are much less developed than we think. And many more people live in poverty in those countries than we think. Our view of poverty depends a lot on who we are, our generation, our profession, and where we live and have lived on Dollar Street.

Money is not the only meaningful measure of poverty. Indeed, large portions of the population, including the poorest, live outside the "money economy". If we take the quality of life into account, some of the reality may look different. To understand the world properly, we need different perspectives. Depending on which measure we use, a country's place in the world rankings may vary. For example, European countries score lower on the Positive Experience Index than Central American countries, even though average income levels are significantly higher in Europe.

Issues of poverty intersect with other issues, such as human rights, gender, environment, climate change, conflict, or urban-rural disparities. Focusing on a single component is easier to take action, but will only address part of the problem.

In 2017, 3.9% of children under 5 died. That's bad. In 1800, almost half of children under 5 died (44%). So we are doing much better after all. In 2015, 14% of the world's adults could neither read nor write. That's too many! In 1960, that figure was 58%. Does it still sound so bad now? It is important to distinguish between a level (for example: bad) and an evolution (for example: better). Things can be both better and bad.

Our World in Data
What are children dying from and what can we do about it?
Analysis

Step by step, extreme poverty in the world is declining. Not on every dimension every year, but as a trend. Although the situation is not rosy and the world still faces enormous challenges, we have made immense progress. Since 1990, over 1 billion people have escaped extreme poverty and infant mortality has fallen by more than half. That is an amazing achievement. But there are still about 700 million people on this planet who struggle to meet their basic needs every day. And more than 6,000 children still die every day from infectious diseases that are perfectly avoidable or treatable. That's bad.

Think of the world as a premature baby in an incubator: Does it make sense to say that the baby's situation is improving? Yes, absolutely. Does it make sense to say that the situation is bad? Yes, absolutely. Does "things are improving" mean that everything is fine and that we should all relax and not worry anymore? No, not at all. Do we have to choose between bad and yet better? Certainly not. It's both. It's both bad and better. Better, and bad, at the same time. This is how we should think about world poverty. Better—so our efforts make a difference and there is reason to be hopeful and persistent. Bad—there's no time to lose, so let's not be complacent, poverty remains one of the world's greatest challenges.

Extreme poverty is declining year after year. That's a fact. Extreme poverty will be eradicated by 2030. That is a myth. Conflict, poor governance, slow economic growth, and a lack of social measures for the weakest keep some populations in a stranglehold and make it difficult to escape. The global pandemic makes this precarious process even more challenging.

Imagine a ladder where the lowest rungs of the ladder represent the countries with the lowest and the highest rungs the countries with the highest per capita income. Climbing this economic development ladder means the end of hunger and misery and generally leads to healthier, happier, and longer-lived people. This is the concept described by Jeffrey Sachs in "The End of Poverty."

Jeffrey Sachs
The End of Poverty
Book

People living in extreme poverty could not set foot on this ladder, and cannot do so on their own. All their efforts are focused on survival. They do not yet have the economic base necessary for further development. They are too poor to save for education, health care, or investment in basic services.

These people need help to get a foot on the first rung of the development ladder. They need basic infrastructure to meet their needs for food and clean water. They need help to acquire education and develop expertise and skills. Only then will they have a real chance of moving forward and being able to offer their children hope for a better future.

Rutger Bregman
Poverty isn't a lack of character, it's a lack of cash
TED Talk

POVERTY IN SUMMARY

- Poverty has a different meaning depending on where you live. National poverty lines give a good indication of relative poverty in a country or region.

- Globally, just under 10% of the world's population (about 700 million people) live in extreme poverty, with an income equivalent to $1.90 per person per day.

- The situation has improved significantly, with over 1 billion people having left extreme poverty behind in the last two decades.

- This improvement was mainly a result of strong economic growth in countries such as China and India.

- The remaining extremely poor are concentrated in several vulnerable areas, characterized by conflict, poor governance, and slow economic growth.

- The global pandemic is having a dramatic impact, sending over 100 million people back into extreme poverty temporarily or permanently.

- The impact of climate change on extreme poverty is increasingly being felt.

- Income inequality is a major problem in many countries, including middle-income and higher-income countries.

- Poverty is complex, has many dimensions, and goes beyond income alone.

- The happiest people do not live in the richest countries; the unhappiest people live in the poorest countries.

- Although the poverty situation worldwide has improved a great deal, it remains bad in certain regions.

- Without help, it is virtually impossible to escape from extreme poverty.

Altruism

"There are those that give with joy, and that joy is their reward."

—Khalil Gibran

VISIONS ON ALTRUISM

Compassion, empathy, altruism, and generosity are related concepts that are often used interchangeably. Where compassion and empathy are feelings, generosity and altruism convert these feelings into actions. The first two form the basis for the last two.

Being compassionate is being aware of the other person's situation, along with the desire to ease the other person's suffering and pursue his or her happiness. In short, compassion lets you understand the suffering of others and think about how you can help.

Empathy is the ability to put yourself in another person's shoes, to put yourself in their situation. It is an emotional response to the suffering of others. Someone with great empathy feels the suffering of others. Empathy is measured by statements such as "I am touched by what other people are going through" or "I feel concerned for people who are less fortunate than I am." In too large doses, empathy can be paralyzing. We would rather have surgery by a surgeon who shows compassion (and is aware of our situation) than by one who is overly empathetic (and reacts emotionally to our pain).

Feelings of compassion and empathy can motivate us to help others. They can give rise to generosity and altruistic behavior if, when faced with another's suffering, you develop the desire to lift or alleviate that suffering.

Generosity is the will and action of freely giving up resources, time, and talents, such as financial donations, volunteering, or using your skills for the good of others or the common good. A generous person doesn't count his efforts to help other people in need or to give someone a boost on their path to success.

Altruism adds another dimension: there is an effort or sacrifice of some sort involved. "I find it important to share my possessions with other people", "I find it important to make an effort for others", or "I strive to work for the good of society" are typical altruistic statements. Altruism is therefore often presented as the opposite of selfishness.

Pure altruism

There is a moral debate about pure versus impure altruism. The pure altruist has no narcissistic consideration and expects nothing in return for his altruistic behavior. He wants to do good, without his contribution being recognized. His donations are, in his eyes, no more valuable than the donations of others.

Effective altruism, of which philosopher Peter Singer is an ardent supporter, is a variation on pure altruism, which advocates giving to organizations that can generate the highest return on the donations they receive. The "Effective Altruism" movement argues that some charities are more effective than others by a factor of 100. That is worthy of discussion and certainly prompts reflection. Giving needs to be more effective and efficient. We can only agree. Charity could certainly use a more businesslike and professional approach. However, reducing it to a purely rational approach ignores personal motives, passion, and commitment that are important or even leading for many people who want to help.

Impure altruism

The impure altruist is looking for a "warm glow" feeling, a pleasant inner sensation that comes from knowing that his gift has contributed to solving a problem for someone else.

Despite the amount of empirical work devoted to it, the underlying mechanism has not yet been fully deciphered. Researchers assimilate it with several mental processes, which are interrelated. The motivation of impure altruists would be driven by an ethical obligation or a preference for the act of giving itself (regardless of whether this is beneficial), by guilt (read: alleviation of guilt), gratitude or to gain or preserve a certain reputation. The circumstances in which altruism leads to a "warm glow" feeling have also been the subject of numerous studies. For example, we know that many people feel better when they buy something for another person rather than for themselves. This feeling is enhanced if they can specifically identify the receiver of the donation (rather than a faceless figure in a statistic) or if the purpose served by their gift has sentimental value to themselves.

Critics point to studies that show the inefficiency of donations motivated by this "warm glow" feeling. Such donors would be more likely to multiply the hedonistic experience of giving by donating a little to different causes, whereas the total amount given would have had a greater impact had it been transferred to one organization.

Does the pleasure of giving ultimately diminish its moral value? Does altruism have to be pure and approached from a purely economic standpoint to be effective? Is it better to help one cause or several? Both forms of altruism are valuable. There is nothing wrong with feeling good about helping others. Just as there is nothing wrong with expecting your donation to be used most effectively.

Reciprocity

Altruism expects nothing in return. Indeed, in the purely altruistic version, expecting anything in return is a moral failing. Yet sometimes the opposite is true. Reciprocity, though sometimes maligned as a typical expression of self-interest, can be an important means of progress. People are naturally cooperative and find solutions more quickly when they work together. But in pure altruism, nothing is ever expected in return. That would pollute altruism. The true altruist rejects all expressions of gratitude. What if one day the receiver is at the door and wants to give something back? The pure altruist should not accept this, because then he would be paid for services rendered (he would become a capitalist!). But isn't this a missed opportunity? Isn't it better to accept the gift after all and "reinvest" it in another good action, thus allowing the cycle of generosity to continue?

Being focused on others is not necessarily an end in itself; the focus should be on finding solutions to problems. "What should we do to help solve this problem as soon as possible?" is at least as important as asking "What should we do to help others?"

Are we altruists?

With our projects, we regularly get questions like "Why are you doing this?" or "What do you get from it?" In the strictly economic sense, we get nothing out of it. Yet we get a lot in return: we learn every day, and the conversations with our children at the kitchen table are extremely fascinating. And yes, we experience a certain satisfaction when we see a new soup kitchen opening its doors. Does this mean that we cannot be considered pure altruists because altruism states that you get nothing in return? Perhaps we are just being generous? What we do, however, costs us money, time, and lots of energy. So are we altruists after all? We don't care what we are called. Like most people, we are not motivated only by pure altruism or just by "warm glow" motives, but by a mix of motivations. We are concerned enough to find solutions to the problems of people who don't know us (and probably never will). Not because we expect anything in return for ourselves, but because it is the right thing to do.

Matthieu Ricard
How to let altruism be your guide
TED Talk

Abigail Marsh
Why some people are more altruistic than others
TED Talk

Elizabeth Dunn
Helping others makes us happier—but it matters how we do it
TED Talk

WHAT WE SHARE WITH OTHER SPECIES

Humans are not the only living beings that act to help others. Many other species cooperate whether or not to achieve a common goal. We have all seen images of the impressive cooperative behavior of certain insects, fish, birds, and monkeys.

A termite colony comprises several castes: the queen and king are the only individuals that reproduce, workers forage and provide food, and soldiers defend the colony from ant attacks. The last two groups exhibit complex social behavior. Some soldiers have jaws so large—they are specialized for defense and attack—that they cannot feed themselves and must be helped by workers. Within a colony of bees, each individual, both male and female, takes responsibility for at least one specific task, such as digging or constructing cells. These are perfectly coordinated with each other. Ant colonies in flooded areas survive by clinging to each other to form a floating raft with each ant taking turns submerging and surfacing. The young are deep inside the sphere, the older ants along the outside, ensuring that the colony survives.

Sardines instinctively form an impressive bait ball as a defense mechanism when threatened: they swarm in a tightly packed spherical formation around a common center, protecting each other. A solitary individual is more easily eaten than one in a large group. Certain species of birds risk their own lives to chase a predator away from another, unrelated bird—but only for conspecifics that exhibit this kind of solidarity behavior as well. Vampire bats share blood with both related and unrelated bats to prevent the one who has had an unsuccessful hunt from starving to death.

Marmoset monkeys spontaneously give food to unrelated monkeys. Brown capuchin monkeys, given the choice of being selfish (by exchanging a token for food) or pro-social (by exchanging another token for food for himself and another monkey), predominantly made the second choice. In another study, chimpanzees helped an unfamiliar human without receiving a reward, even when they had to make a physical effort to help. Then again, in yet another study, chimpanzees helped conspecifics complete a task to receive a food reward, even when they had already gotten theirs. They did this automatically and voluntarily, without being asked.

In these and many other examples, various species help each other. However, one aspect seems to be unique to human beings: anonymously giving resources, time, and even sperm or organs to help strangers they will never meet. We have not yet observed this kind of altruistic behavior in any non-human species.

Although humans are an animal at the very top of the food chain and are capable of extreme aggression, it is even more true that we are genetically programmed to be cooperative and generous. Cooperation is the defining characteristic of human society. Although the daily portion of violence in the news bulletin suggests otherwise, aggression is the exception, not the rule (which is why it's news).

Frans de Waal
Moral behavior in animals
TED Talk

INNATE OR
LEARNED?

This brings us to whether altruism is innate or rather learned. Several studies show that altruistic behavior is present in very young children, even before they can speak. Toddlers have an innate urge to cooperate and help others. They give an object to a person who can't reach it themselves, divide toys roughly equally among themselves (even if it means giving something up), or proactively pick up an object that someone accidentally drops. They exhibit these behaviors spontaneously, with no encouragement, and not just in the presence of their parents, which suggests that the urge to help is intrinsically motivated. One study has even shown that young toddlers not only help others but also help empathically (such as giving a toy to a sad researcher) and even altruistically (such as giving their favorite toy to a sad researcher). This, according to Harvard professor Felix Warneken, proves that generosity and altruism are deeply ingrained in human nature and goes directly against social science theories and explanations that assume "rational egoism"—that everything humans do is ultimately driven by calculated self-interest.

This urge to help and cooperate is tempered as children get older and their giving behavior becomes more selective and nuanced. Besides general social factors, research shows that the culture in which a person grows up has a major influence. A study of children and adults from six different societies —the United States, Fiji, the Central African Republic, Namibia, Ecuador, and Australia— showed that very young children behaved in much the same way in all cultures. Generous behavior only began to differ during the preschool years, when children seemed to conform to the norms of the adults in their societies. This suggests that although young children share a strong and universal tendency toward generosity, cultural forces can temper this impulse.

Societies in which generosity and altruism are encouraged will produce people who are more generous than societies where this is not the case. Young people who have been raised by parents showing the right example will be more generous themselves once adults, sometimes without even realizing it. This is reinforced when parents talk to their children about the importance of this type of behavior, make them aware of the impact of their actions, and give their children the opportunity to be useful to others.

Developing a sense of justice and altruistic behavior is like learning a language. We are genetically equipped with brains that are predisposed to it, but you also need to be talked to or you won't learn it.

Nurture or lose

Even as adults, we often have an initial impulse to be altruistic, but we just as often talk ourselves out of it, usually for absurd reasons. For example, when we see a homeless woman trying to keep warm in the winter cold, our first thought may be to give her a winter coat we haven't worn in a long time. But then an inner dialogue starts. "Maybe I'll want to wear it one day" or "when I come back with the coat she won't be here anymore" or even "someone else will surely give her a coat." We override our natural tendency to be generous by relying too much on the "thinking" parts of our brain. Instead of following our natural impulses, we come up with all kinds of far-fetched reasons and excuses why we shouldn't help.

We must become aware of this tendency and restore the balance between our empathic and logical ability to judge whether we should be generous. The lady who buys a coffee for the homeless man on Main Street is by nature an empathetic person. She has learned that giving and caring for others is part of life. She tried it and it felt good. She is doing it again, and she is considering it more and more normal. She lives in a cycle of generosity that is maintained by a combination of giving and receiving, determined by nature and her upbringing. Her logical thinking skills help her assess the situation and risks and weigh the pros and cons. She does not put herself at risk, the hot coffee and her gesture mean a lot to the man, and it only costs her a few euros or dollars. Let's do it. Empathy makes her help, logic keeps her safe and protected.

The brain rewards you with a shot of dopamine when you are generous. That wonderful "feel good" hormone sizzles through your bloodstream when you follow your altruistic instinct. It's like a boomerang: give to someone in need and the joy will bounce right back to you as a warm, fuzzy feeling of reward and pleasure.

We are designed and born with a level of neural empathy. This is reinforced when, as teenagers, we are raised by the rest of the herd to help others. The secret is to nurture this capital in our young people and teach them to see altruism as a normal and necessary part of life. Even if we could use some gentle reminders from time to time.

An old Cherokee Indian gives advice to his grandson. "*There is a fight going on inside me,*" he tells the boy. "*It is a terrible fight between two wolves. One is Evil—he is hatred, anger, greed, envy, arrogance, resentment, avarice, and cowardice. The other is Good— he is happiness, joy, serenity, love, kindness, compassion, hope, humility, generosity, truthfulness, and trust. They also fight in you and everyone else.*"
The child thinks about it for a minute and asks his grandfather, "*Which wolf will win?*"
To which the old Cherokee simply replies, "*The one you feed.*"

This is the romantic version that circulates the most on the Internet. The story, as originally told by the Native Americans, is a little more nuanced. If you only feed the good wolf, the evil one will become so hungry that it will attack in every way possible and try to kill the good one. The trick is to tame the evil one so that both can live together in harmony.

Happify
The story of the two wolves
Video

WE ARE SO 'WEIRD'

Complete the following sentence in 5 different ways: "I'm _____". If you answered with words like "curious", "handsome", "a consultant", or "a marathon runner", then you are almost certainly "WEIRD". If you thought more like "son of Ronny" or "part of the fifth generation of Rouffaer's from Roosdaal", then you are more in line with most of the world's population. At least according to Joseph Henrich, in his book "The Weirdest People in the World" about the "Western, well-Educated, Industrialized, Rich and Democratic"—or "WEIRD"—mentality.

The way people living in 'non-WEIRD' societies view the world is often very different from our own 'WEIRD' worldview. For example, some cultures share more. Members of the #Akhoe Hai//om community in Namibia were hunter-gatherers until three generations ago. Should you live there, anything that can be shared is as much yours as mine. I could tell you to give me "my" shoes, and the fact that you are currently wearing them doesn't matter. The natural result is that everyone has about the same amount of everything.

Many of the psychological research and surveys only study "Weirdos". Generalizing their conclusions to non-WEIRD populations is dangerous. To assume that concepts that apply in our cultural context apply everywhere is wrong. It is even more wrong if we attach a value judgment to what is right according to our "WEIRD" standards. For example, in our view, we should reward people based on their performance (and sometimes their effort). If I put in (much) more effort, I am rewarded (much) more. That seems fair. But #Akhoe Hai//om children usually divide things equally, regardless of who contributed how much. That evokes an emotional reaction of "unfairness" in us. But depending on where you were born and raised, this reaction can be very different. And different does not mean wrong or bad.

The Cultural Fixation Index (CFST) offers an interesting look at how cultural differences affect our worldview. The index determines the cultural distance between countries or regions by comparing the value judgments of their populations on various topics such as politics (e.g., views on democracy), social relationships (e.g., child education), religious norms and traditions, sex, finance, environment, science and innovation, arts and creativity, sports and recreation, media, and consumer society. Theoretically, CFST values can range from 0 to 1. The closer to zero, the smaller the cultural differences. "1" would mean that the countries being compared culturally are the exact opposite of each other in every aspect considered.

Figure 18 shows the cultural "distance" between the Netherlands and several countries (figures for Belgium are not currently available). Germany is the most culturally similar, and Egypt is the most different. Note that countries that are about equally different from the Netherlands do not necessarily have similar cultures among themselves. South Africa and China both have a CFST value of about 0.15 relative to the Netherlands and yet a similar cultural distance between them.

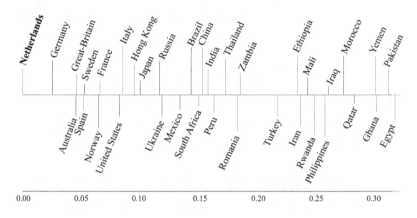

Figure 18: The cultural distance between the Netherlands and other countries
(Source: chart created based on data available from www.culturaldistance.com)

Henrich and his colleagues developed an index for two countries often regarded as each other's cultural opposites: the United States and China. The American scale is an indicator of a country's cultural "distance" from the United States. The Chinese scale is an indicator of cultural "distance" from China. All values on both scales are less than 0.3. This is consistent with findings of other research showing that there are more similarities than differences between cultures. But that does not mean that relatively small differences cannot be very relevant. Remember that only 4% of our genes differ from those of chimpanzees!

This technique can also examine cultural differences between regions within countries, between social classes, between age groups, or between any other groupings. For example, it is interesting to note that cultural differences between regions of the United States are significantly smaller than those within the European Union, China, or India. So while talking about "the" American is relatively OK, the image of "the" European, "the" Chinese, and "the" Indian is very much less pertinent because of the significant regional differences within these regions or countries.

What does this mean for us? Simply put, what WEIRD people (like most of us reading this book) consider good or bad, poor or rich, honest or dishonest, selfish or altruistic, generous or not generous,... is perhaps (read: probably) very different from what non-WEIRD people think. The context in which we live strongly influences the way we think about the world and about certain life questions in particular. It is tempting and dangerous to assume that our view is the only correct one and to judge or even condemn others when their ideas differ from ours. And that's important to keep in mind if you want to help others.

Culturaldistance.com
To compare the cultural distance between
countries
Data

(NOT) THE PRIVILEGE OF THE RICH

Are the people of some countries more generous than those of others? Is generosity determined by where you are born? Is altruism a privilege of wealthier countries? The Charities Aid Foundation (CAF) World Giving Index determines the 10 most and least generous nations, based on data collected by Gallup in 128 countries from 2009 to 2018. Participants were asked if they had helped a stranger, given money to, or volunteered for a charity in the month before the survey. With all the bad news that floods us daily, you may be surprised at how many people around the world are actively working to make this world a better place. The report shows that during the past decade, nearly 1 billion people volunteered time to an organization, nearly 1.4 billion people donated money to charity and over 2 billion people helped a stranger.

As stated in Figure 19, the United States emerged as the most generous country over the past decade, with an overall score of 58%. Seven of the world's wealthiest countries were also in the top 10, including New Zealand in third place and Australia in fourth. Less affluent countries such as Myanmar, Sri Lanka, and Indonesia also made it into the top 10. Belgium only came in at place 42, well behind the Netherlands (8), Germany (18), and Luxembourg (28), but ahead of France (66).

	CAF World Giving Index ranking	CAF World Giving Index score (%)	% that has helped a stranger who needed help	% that has donated money to a charity	% that has volunteered time to an organization
United States	1	58%	72%	61%	42%
Myanmar	2	58%	49%	81%	43%
New Zealand	3	57%	64%	65%	41%
Australia	4	56%	64%	68%	37%
Ireland	5	56%	62%	69%	38%
Canada	6	55%	64%	63%	37%
United Kingdom	7	54%	60%	71%	30%
Netherlands	8	53%	53%	71%	36%
Sri Lanka	9	51%	55%	50%	46%
Indonesia	10	50%	42%	69%	40%
Belgium	42	36%	44%	39%	25%

Figure 19: Top 10 countries in the CAF World Giving Index Ranking (2019)
(Source: 2019 CAF World Giving Index rapport)

The list offers some interesting insights, including::

- New Zealand was the only country to appear in the top 10 on the three dimensions on which people were surveyed, and China was the only country consistently in the bottom 10.

- In the top 20 are several developing or even poor countries (e.g., Myanmar, Kenya, and Indonesia) while several "rich" countries are near the bottom of the list (e.g. Japan at position 107).

Generosity and altruism can have different faces from country to country (people in Africa, for example, more readily help a person they don't know than people from former Eastern Europe or Asia). Yet, at first glance, there is no "secret" ingredient. Rather, there seems to be a combination of reasons that make the people of one country more generous than those of another. Regardless of which country you think should be #1, Gallup's survey confirms you don't have to be rich to be generous. Some countries where people have far fewer resources (like Indonesia, Kenya, and Myanmar) are at the top of the list (in fact, Indonesia was #1 in 2018, Myanmar the four previous years). Countries like Haiti and Nigeria are also in the top 20. Of the 19 countries that make up the G20 along with the European Union (together accounting for about 90% of world production and 80% of world trade), only 6 are in the top 40 on the list. So, generosity is not the prerogative of "rich" or "democratic" countries. If income is not at the root of generosity and altruism, what is?

Charities Aid Foundation
2019 CAF World Giving Index
Report

Paul Hawken
Blessed unrest
Video

THE ROLE OF
RELIGION

Christianity is the largest religion worldwide, with over two billion followers. The second most practiced religion is Islam, with an estimated 1.8 billion followers. Hinduism, one of the oldest religions with beliefs and practices dating back at least to 1500 before our era, follows in place three with about 1.1 billion followers. The fourth most practiced religion is Buddhism, with some 500 million followers worldwide. There is debate whether Buddhism is a religion —no God is worshipped—or a philosophical movement or "teaching" with moral precepts for those who want to become good people. For the context of this book, however, this discussion is of little relevance.

In all these religions, we see a common thread of recognition for people in need and guidelines on how to morally and effectively address the problems of poverty, isolation, and oppression. All embrace the concept of "generosity." For Christians, charity is central. In Islam, "īthār" (altruism) stands for preferring others to oneself. Mohandas Gandhi exemplified the traditional Hindu focus on altruism. Gandhi was even given the title Mahatma ("honored person" or "sage") in recognition of his remarkable efforts to help others. Finally, in Buddhism, people are encouraged to direct love and compassion toward others, which is said to promote happiness. Most other religions (such as Sikhism and Judaism) also consider generosity an essential virtue.

Religion plays a major role in charity, both as a motivator and as an actor on the ground. While there is criticism of some religious aid organizations that have been accused of discrimination or conversion in exchange for aid, we cannot deny that they continue to play an important role in the fight against poverty and oppression in a wide range of vulnerable areas.

Since the three "most generous" countries on the list have different predominant religions, religion does not appear at first glance to be a distinguishing factor. All religions appear to influence generosity to a greater or lesser extent. However, how this occurs and how followers are encouraged to be generous differs. For example, Myanmar and Sri Lanka have many Theravada Buddhists for whom small, frequent gifts to monks as alms, food, medicine, and clothing are the norm in exchange for teaching and other services. This may have contributed to the historically high generosity scores of both countries.

Christianity

Charity is central to Christianity and is much more than giving alms to the poorest. While Christians accept that helping the poor and needy is a moral and religious obligation, it goes much further. Charity is love. Christians believe that God's love and generosity toward humanity moves and inspires us to love and be generous in response. This love for others is expressed as "solidarity" with those in need. When Christians live by this principle, they do so not out of condescending pity, but out of a commitment to a common good, so that each person can reach his full potential. For Christians, charity is much more radical and profound than simply giving "left over." They believe that everything they have is a gift from God and does not belong to them alone. It should be shared if there is someone who needs it more. Christianity has historically established charitable institutions, such as schools, hospitals, and social service agencies, which remain strong pillars in many of the poorest communities today.

Islam

The two types of charity that emerge in the texts of the Qur'an are Zakat, a mandatory alms tax for the benefit of the poor, and Sadaq, a voluntary gift, which is recommended to every Muslim. Zakat is one of the five pillars of Islam, alongside the confession of faith, daily prayer, fasting, and pilgrimage. It is an important aspect of the lives of Muslims, regardless of their social status. Muslims who are more successful and resourceful are more likely to make monetary donations, while others may donate their time. The prayers of those who do not pay their Zakat are not accepted within Islam. There is no specific amount stipulated, but the expectation is usually that one gives 2.5% of their annual income. Because of the obligatory nature of Zakat, it can be argued that it is not an act of generosity or altruism. However, the terms Zakat and Sadaq are often used interchangeably. Both involve donations to those in need and, regardless of whether one gives out of obligation or free will, it is assumed that the act is selfless and reflects the pure intention of the donor.

Poor communities, institutions, and organizations in certain countries (such as Afghanistan and Somalia) currently live solely on Zakat money. Schools and orphanages actively collect Zakat donations annually, especially during the month of Ramadan. Zakat makes Islam the first welfare system in history to redistribute a portion of the wealth of the rich to the poor as a way of achieving social justice. The mosque or state collects and administers the donations and then distributes them to the communities that need them most. Zakat also plays an important developmental role in Islamic society. For example, Zakat is used for various projects that create jobs and opportunities to help the poor become self-sufficient. Muslims are discouraged from giving to the poor who can work, as this fosters dependency and inhibits development and growth. Creating jobs and thus allowing the poor to earn an income is, according to most Muslims, much more effective in combating poverty than giving them alms.

Sadaq is a form of voluntary charity for those who wish to give more than their obligatory Zakat. This can be money, time, food, or efforts and can be given at any time (not just during Ramadan), both by the rich and by the poor. Sadaq is usually given in secret, to respect the receiver's feelings and preserve their identity.

Both forms of charity are a way to eliminate social inequalities and thus ensure equality and social justice. The Muslim community places great value on hard work, education, and giving back to the community. All these are crucial in the fight against poverty.

Hinduism

For Hindus, giving and charity, better known as *Dana*, are essential to one's *Dharma*, or religious duty. Hindus are expected to give freely to ensure that they fulfill their Dharma. They believe that this will ultimately affect their *Karma*, that "all thoughts and actions have consequences in this or the next life." Since Hindus believe in reincarnation and that their actions in this life will affect their next life, it is common to give freely. Giving and charity are thus essential aspects of Hindu tradition, culture, religion, and life. For example, Hindus find it normal to take responsibility for family members (in the broadest sense) who are struggling.

Followers of Hinduism are also expected to work for the good of society. One example is the sharing of food, better known to Hindus as *Annadan*. This tradition calls on Hindus to share their food with unexpected visitors who happen to pass by. The orthodox tradition calls on the heads of the family not to eat themselves until they have offered the food to their family members, gods, ancestors, and any mendicant. According to tradition, he is expected to go out and proclaim before each meal, "Is anyone hungry? Be welcome!" To this day, offering food to the hungry is considered one of the greatest gifts in India. Although Annadan is not as common as it used to be, this selfless act of giving is still highly respected in India. Many Indian charities still offer meals to the poor. Besides Annadan, several other forms of charity exist among Hindus, such as *Vastradan* (giving clothes) and *Patradan* (donating utensils).

For Hindus, giving is at the core of their belief system. This is not something they choose to do, but something they believe they must do; it is their duty. They view charity and giving as responsibilities, not as acts of generosity.

Buddhism

Buddhism also has a different view of giving than the Western tradition. Buddhism sees giving not only as a virtue but as a way of life to achieve true enlightenment, the ultimate goal of Buddhism. The omnipresence of giving and of generosity strikes anyone who delves into Buddhism. Starting with the Buddha, this tradition has always emphasized that an outstretched hand and an open heart are essential if one is to make spiritual progress.

In Buddhism, giving is based on what the recipient needs most. This ranges from the most basic material things, such as food, clothing, and shelter, to things that require more from the giver, such as advice, education, or even someone's life. The Buddhist tradition of giving recognizes that there is a range of motivations, from purely transactional (when I get something back for what I give) to transcendent (when giving means overcoming selfishness). Any of these motivations are accepted, as long as they find their source in purity, where we give solely for the sake of giving.

The act of giving brings happiness in the future, by the laws of karma taught by the Buddha. Good deeds will give rise to good consequences and bad deeds to bad consequences. The idea is to create as much good karma as possible by keeping one's mind pure when giving, choosing the worthiest receiver, and offering the most appropriate and generous gifts one can afford.

Since there is great emphasis in Buddhism on the path to discovery or enlightenment, generosity is seen as a process in one's existence. This process, which must be maintained, is many times more important than giving itself. In Buddhism, giving benefits the giver from a spiritual perspective and the receiver from a pragmatic perspective. It tops the list of the ten perfections or qualities that lead a person to enlightenment, underscoring the importance of generosity in the life of a Buddhist practitioner.

In Buddhism, generosity is not viewed through an economic lens. The gift of service and the gift of teaching are considered of greater value than the gift of wealth or material possessions. Social harmony is achieved through generosity, kindness, service, and equal treatment. Therefore, generosity is practiced not only for the sake of those in need or for the sake of humanity but for the sake of the universal. For Buddhists, generosity cannot be considered a separate act. This may explain why there are no known Buddhist philanthropic organizations or foundations. Generosity must come from within and become a part of one's being, as opposed to an act or gesture that one performs externally. For Buddhists, giving is an act of being rather than an act of doing.

THE SOCIAL
CONTEXT

Besides the influence of religion, the context and situation in which society finds itself also play a significant role in the generosity of a population. Residents of countries ravaged by conflict (e.g., Yemen) or facing serious economic problems (e.g., Venezuela) are less generous and exhibit less altruistic behavior, especially toward people who are not part of their group. The circumstances force them to focus on their survival, which is quite understandable.

Also, charity is a fairly new concept in countries with a young civil society or where the relationship between the state and this civil society is still shaky. Two good examples of countries where altruistic behavior has only recently taken off are Russia and China.

Russia

Generosity and charity are relatively new in Russia. For seventy years of communism, charity was demeaning to the receiver. It was the responsibility of the state to provide for all needs, material and spiritual, and there was no reason for the common individual to interfere. It was only after the fall of the Soviet Union that giving and caring for the less fortunate came back into focus. In the early 1990s, wealthy families and large corporations that were primarily connected to specific cities or regions in the company's vicinity established foundations. Gifts from the middle class were very low; five years before, they were virtually non-existent.

Interesting contrast between capitalist and communist thinking soon emerged. The new rich in Russia argue they owe society nothing, but the poor think charity is the duty of the rich and there is a general hostility to individual wealth. As expected, there is very little charitable giving by the general population; according to the World Giving Index, only six percent of Russians donate regularly.

Charity in Russia differs from that in other countries in several ways. First, almost all donations remain in Russia. Russian philanthropists are primarily concerned with solving domestic problems. In addition, trust in the charity sector is very low because of a lack of transparency and openness, so aid is mostly given directly to people in need or state-run institutions, such as orphanages. Finally, secular rather than religious charities receive the vast majority of donations.

Since the beginning of this century, the generosity of the middle class has increased significantly, but it remains very difficult for non-governmental organizations to gain a foothold in Russia.

China

For years, China has also dangled at the bottom of the list of the most generous countries on the World Giving Index. To illustrate, in 2012, total charitable donations in China were $13.2 billion, or a mere 4 percent of all U.S. donations. Although a major natural disaster (such as the devastating Sichuan earthquake in 2008) can trigger a surge of support, conscious, voluntary action for the welfare of others is not yet an integral part of the life of the average Chinese. Until recently, Chinese society even discriminated against charity work. When charity icon Yao Li founded the country's first charity school for children of migrant workers in 2004, she was called a fraud.

Establishing and registering a "social organization" as a non-profit was complicated because of an unfriendly political and policy environment. To establish a local foundation, an initial fund of RMB 2 million (over 250,000 euros) was required. In addition, institutions had to join an official body, which meant they lost autonomy in managing their funds or had to pay corporate taxes.

In 2016, after many years of debate, the National People's Congress passed a charity law that removed several restrictions, paving the way for a revival of the charity sector in China. There is still some disagreement about the role of charity in society, but the number of donations and registered organizations increases dramatically. Meanwhile, China's super-rich are competing in terms of generosity in various fields: from nature conservation and fighting climate change to supporting early childhood education.

Charity, however, remains a relatively recent phenomenon in China and still lags far behind most other countries. But the trend change seems to be underway.

THE CULTURAL DIMENSION

The culture of a region or a population may have the greatest impact on the latter's altruistic behavior. The concepts of giving and generosity are not limited to Western traditions. Cooperation, charity, and solidarity with those in need are the norm rather than the exception in most countries and cultures, and that is good news. Human beings are social creatures by nature, and generosity is in many places the lubricant that keeps the engine of society running. In different cultures, this is expressed in different ways. What follows are some illustrations and specific examples from different parts of the world of how culture influences cooperation and generosity. The list is, of course, much longer and deserves a book in itself.

Ubuntu

Nkosikho Mbele was a pump attendant at a gas station in Khayelitsha. When a white woman noticed that she had forgotten her credit card at home and had no cash on her, he stepped up to her and without being asked, gave her

100 rand to fill up. In a country with a large racial divide like South Africa, this is even more unexpected. The media picked up the story and when asked why he did not want to be paid back he replied "when you do something for someone, no matter how small it is, do it from your heart, not to want something in return". This is exactly what ubuntu is about.

In the Xhosa language, the term ubuntu refers to "humanity." In Kinyarwanda, it stands for "generosity." It is a concept that exists in almost all Bantu languages of Africa and encompasses the concept of community and interdependence between people. Ubuntu is clearly illustrated in Zulu and Bantu by the proverb "Umuntu, ngumuntu, ngabantu," which can be translated as "the individual is an individual only because of other individuals." In other words, "I am because you are".

Ubuntu is a very simple but powerful concept, and it includes sharing, honesty, hospitality, caring, truthfulness, and all the good you can think of. Ubuntu simply means that we are all one family. "I am who I am because of who we all are." As a human being, I cannot live in isolation. I need other people to be human. Without other people I could not walk, talk, act and learn—I could not live. I learned everything from other people. We are all connected and we cannot be truly happy unless others are also happy. That is the basic meaning of ubuntu. Ubuntu doesn't mean you can't be rich. You can be rich, but only by positive means, not at the expense of others. You don't have to cheat or oppress others to be rich. Your wealth must have a positive impact on others and on the society in which you live.

The Archbishop of Cape Town, leader of the anti-apartheid movement, and Nobel prize winner Desmond Tutu has always been an ardent advocate of ubuntu and summed up the philosophy as follows, "It is the essence of being human. It speaks of the fact that my humanity is inseparable from yours. It speaks of wholeness, it speaks of compassion. People with ubuntu feel bad when others are humiliated, oppressed, or treated as if they are less than who they are. Ubuntu gives people resilience, allowing them to survive and continue to exist as human beings despite all attempts to dehumanize them." Ubuntu is a way of life. It is a key explanation why residents of many African countries readily help people they do not know.

Nelson Mandela
The Ubuntu Experience
Video

Boyd Varty
What I learned from Nelson Mandela
TED Talk

Desmond Tutu
Who we are: Human uniqueness and the African spirit of Ubuntu
Video

Bayanihan

The Philippines has a long tradition of giving and volunteerism. Bayanihan, working together towards a common goal for the benefit of the entire community, is one of the country's core values.

The origin of the term Bayanihan goes back to a common tradition in Philippine cities in which community members volunteered to help a family move their stilt house to a new place—literally. Volunteers lifted and carried the house, placed on a frame of bamboo poles. Of course, with stone houses, this became a little more difficult, but the philosophy remained and is still alive.

In times of emergency, the Bayanihan philosophy encourages local people to unite, support victims, and rebuild the community. It explains why Dr. Cua, a doctor who worked in the safe confines of a private hospital in Manila, braved the debris-strewn roads at the risk of her own life to offer help after the passage of Hurricane Haiyan in 2013. "*How could I go on with my life and not go there when I knew people were suffering and I could help?*"

Arihant Publications
Bayanihan: the spirit of community
Video

La Rifa

Although many believe Colombia is one of the most dangerous countries in the world, the situation is not as precarious as the media portray it. Colombia is known for its friendly culture and its solidarity. Whenever a member of the community faces adversity, for example, when the main breadwinner of the family is in prison, loses his job, or dies, the community springs into action. Often a kind of lottery or raffle is organized, called "La Rifa".

The leader of the community, usually an older man, collects donations from the members of the group. In Colombian culture, items such as electric blenders or radios are luxury items that are large donations. He raffles these items among community members. Everyone likes to take part in La Rifa, not only because they can win a great prize, but also because they know the proceeds will benefit a community member in need. In addition, the leader goes door to door to collect donations for the family or person in need. Since the average monthly wage of a Colombian is rather low, these consist mainly of food and basic commodities.

In Colombian culture, there is a strong emphasis on generosity within the community and donating one's time and efforts to help other members. These acts of generosity are temporary, and emphasis is placed on the concept of reciprocity. Once the community member has recovered, he returns help to those who helped him.

Mahiber

In Ethiopia, an East African country, becoming a member of a Mahiber ("association") is one of the most important forms of social interaction people have with each other. It is a traditional organization that provides a safety net for its members. The group meets regularly, usually every month. These meetings are rarely formal and are organized at members' homes. The host is expected to provide a meal or snacks, depending on the time of day. Part of the meeting is devoted to discussing important issues, and the rest is spent socializing. Money collected at each meeting is saved and used when a member needs help. When an individual cannot contribute financially, he will instead do manual labor such as helping the host prepare for the meeting.

Members receive support from their Mahiber in the event of a death in the family. This financial help depends on the kinship of the deceased. For example, a larger amount is paid out when someone loses a husband or wife than if it was a brother or sister. In addition, the other members of the Mahiber help serve afternoon and evening meals to guests of the grieving family for three days. In doing so, the Mahiber relieves the family of all practical concerns and gives them time to mourn the loss of their loved one.

Although it may seem insignificant, the contribution of a Mahiber to the lives of individuals, and society, is priceless. It not only provides people with the material and physical support they need during difficult times but also gives people the opportunity to share good times and bad times with each other.

Giri

Giri is an important Japanese value that refers to the "social obligation" and the duty to act as expected by society. The Japanese place a high value on politeness and gratitude. Children show kindness and respect to their parents and to people outside their homes to emphasize the dignity of their parents and ancestors. Japanese are essentially loyal only to their immediate family. They are group-oriented and they focus on who they know rather than who they do not know. Companies only care for their employees and not for the community in which they are located. Public charity or donations are usually seen in Japan as the responsibility of the government and not of individuals. Japanese philanthropy is focused on factors that benefit their economic status, such as science and technology. Giving is primarily aimed at making a profit and building economic and social status. It is rare for Japanese to donate to organizations or people they do not know because when they give something, they expect something in return. They keep track of the value of the gifts they receive and, on a special occasion, return an equivalent gift. Charity is an uncommon practice for most Japanese and is not part of their culture, in fact, the word does not exist in Japanese.

Caridad

In Honduras, one of the poorest countries in the Western Hemisphere, children learn at an early age that "la Caridad empieza en la casa" (charity begins at home). The family is very important to Latin Americans. If a family member needs help, the rest of the family joins forces to help him or her. For example, primary education is free and the responsibility of the government. Parents who want their children to continue studying must pay for registration, books, and uniforms. Older children who have completed their education and gone to work are expected to contribute financially to the tuition costs of their siblings. Since there is no social safety net for seniors, children take care of their aging parents. In Honduras, helping is considered everyone's moral duty.

Community kitchens

Everybody knows community kitchens or comedores populares in Peru. Women established these types of kitchens in the late 1960s to mitigate the effects of economic crises by preparing meals for small children and sick members of the community. Migrants from rural areas brought this tradition to the slums of Lima. Even today, "olla comuns" or community kitchens help the weakest members of the community.

PERSONAL
MOTIVATIONS

Besides the social, religious, cultural, and societal context in which a person lives, many personal elements also determine one's altruistic behavior. The influence of a person's socioeconomic status on generosity is complex: some studies show that wealthier people are more generous than poorer ones, and other studies point to the opposite. The conflicting conclusions depend on the context in which the studies took place and factors such as timing. It is difficult for a poorer person to make a financial donation at the end of the month.

For convenience, we will divide personal motivators into intrinsic and extrinsic motivators. Intrinsic motivation comes from within, while extrinsic motivation has an external origin. When you are intrinsically motivated, you take part in an activity because you enjoy it and derive personal satisfaction from it. When you are extrinsically motivated, you act to get an external reward or to avoid potential problems. You may be motivated because you want to positively affect the lives of those around you. You may also be motivated because the social group to which you belong expects it from you.

Pleasure
Purpose
Growth
Interest
Passion

Rewards
Expectations
Obligation
Fear
Acceptance

Figure 20: Intrinsic versus extrinsic motivators for altruistic behavior

Intrinsic motivators

Feelings of empathy, compassion, and other emotions can motivate us to help others. Certain personality traits, such as humility and leniency, are associated with greater generosity, and a person's tendency to exhibit altruistic behavior may be considered a personality trait in itself. A person's values, morals, and sense of duty may also influence their willingness to be generous.

Some people have a desire to change the way they or other people think and feel. They act and engage in interactions to make themselves and those around them feel better. A typical example is someone motivated to work for a non-profit or volunteer in a soup kitchen because they feel good when they make others feel good. Others are more likely to be motivated by the sense of accomplishment they get when they complete a task or when they (help to) solve a problem for a person or group of people. Still, others are driven by an internal force they cannot explain. Their actions are motivated by deep physiological primal feelings that they cannot ignore, no matter how hard they try. Someone who jumps into the water to save a child usually does so out of reflex, without thinking about it. They don't ask themselves the question "should I do this?", they just do it and think it's the most normal thing in the world.

Extrinsic motivators

Other people are motivated more by some form of reward than by the achievement of the goal itself. In quite a few countries, for example, there are tax incentives to encourage people to donate. Or certain organizations raffle off fun prizes among people who support them or organize a charity auction. While this can spur a group of people into action, it can also lead to conflicts with the ethical and cultural values of certain donors. Some supporters will drop out if they see this type of incentive as a payment rather than a gesture of gratitude.

The reverse motivation also exists. Some people want to avoid negative consequences or "buy off" a sense of guilt and are thus driven to action.

Finally, people are social beings and are motivated by social factors such as acceptance and belonging. We have an innate desire to connect with others, and this type of social motivation causes us to seek connections by contributing to a social group. Although it may seem that the motivation comes from within, acceptance by others is often the driving factor.

Which one is the best?

Intrinsic motivation is usually more sustainable than extrinsic motivation because it is under your control. Extrinsic motivation depends on external factors (stimuli, fear, or expectations). It may seem that these two types of motivation are opposed to each other, while both can be perfectly complementary. An interesting study by the Polish researcher Sokolowski found that people most often engage in activities such as volunteering and giving because someone showed them the example. This (external) social motivation triggered participation in these activities, which then had a positive effect on the individual's attitudes, and ultimately encouraged further action. Exposing young people to the sometimes harrowing living conditions of underprivileged age-mates can challenge their habits and thinking patterns and lead to a complete attitude change. Almost no one is motivated by only internal or external motivators. Finding the right balance between the two is the best strategy and will ultimately increase your intrinsic altruistic capacity.

When in doubt, trust your intuition, go with your gut, and do what feels right. If it feels right, don't argue with yourself—keep doing it.

THE UNEXPECTED EXTRAS

Who doesn't love an altruistic person? Someone who helps us in times of need, gives us advice when we have a problem or is just nice when we need it. Altruism is good for those on the receiving end, but also seems to have benefits for those who exhibit this type of behavior, provided it's their own choice.

Many studies point to the positive effects on the giver. Giving social support (time, effort, money, or goods) is linked to better overall health in older adults, and volunteering is associated with longer life spans. Altruism appears to be particularly strongly associated with psychological health and well-being. Other studies have shown a link between altruism and happiness and associate altruism with reducing the risk of burnout and better and longer-lasting relationships.

Altruism and health

Volunteering may be a good way to increase physical activity in older adults who are primarily inactive—and physical activity has been linked to better health. The question is, of course, what is the cause and what is the effect? Does volunteering lead to better health or do healthy people volunteer more?

A recent study followed 300,000 married couples (including 100,000 who volunteered regularly) for 33 months. It examined whether the risk of death was different between volunteers and their spouses who did not volunteer. The study found that volunteers generally had a lower risk of death than their partners, even though they lived in the same household and had similar life hygiene. Among the non-volunteers, this did not appear to be the case. While this is not conclusive evidence, it is at least a sign that volunteering may have a causal relationship with longer life expectancy.

Another study examined the impact of motives for volunteering on mortality risk. This study found that respondents who volunteered had a lower risk of dying within four years, especially those who volunteered more regularly and frequently. However, volunteering was not always favorably related to mortality risk. People who cited selfish motives for their volunteer work had a similar mortality risk as non-volunteers. In contrast, volunteers who cited altruistic motives had a lower mortality risk (even considering all other factors that might have an influence, such as age, gender, and health). This study is complementary to the existing literature on the powerful effects of social interactions and volunteering on health and, to our knowledge, is the first study to examine the effect of motives on volunteers' subsequent mortality. Volunteers live longer than non-volunteers, but only if they volunteer for altruistic reasons.

Sara Konrath, one of the study's authors, explains this seemingly odd association. People who volunteer for non-altruistic reasons (e.g., to command admiration or seek recognition) would be more likely to experience this as a type of work from which they hope to derive personal benefit. Thus, their volunteering would be psychologically about the same as a job done to earn money, resulting in stress. In contrast, people who sincerely volunteer, without ulterior motives, to help others would experience less stress. Volunteering is a source of satisfaction and makes that person happier. And it is generally accepted that happy people live longer than unhappy people.

The exact explanation, of course, remains puzzling. Perhaps the people who did not volunteer were in poor health, which would explain why they did not start helping others —and which would explain a higher mortality rate. However, this does not explain why non-altruistic volunteers have a similar mortality rate to non-volunteers.

Suppose it's been a rough day and you could use a little boost. You receive 100 dollars and are asked to divide it between yourself and the local food bank. That was the question to the participants in a study at the University of Oregon. The results of the MRI scans showed that when participants gave the full amount to the food bank, they felt a sense of accomplishment—similar to that of a delicious meal or viewing a beautiful piece of art. At first glance, it seems surprising that people get a reward when they donate money, especially from an economic perspective. People experience even more brain activity when they give voluntarily. This is caused by the "pleasure" systems in our brains that are activated when we help others. The knowledge that we have acted to improve the life of another is enough to boost our feelings of self-worth and meaning. Some psychologists say that pro-social spending distracts the giver from his own problems and shifts the focus to greater hope and optimism. When this activity is done over an extended period, it actively reduces exposure to stress hormones and boosts immunity.

There are many ways to give altruistically. Sharing time or expertise. Donating money, goods, or services. These are all proven methods of uplifting the spirit and boosting morale. The major determinant of this emotional reward is altruism itself. People who are told to engage in altruistic behavior— those who do not feel they have a choice—are much less likely to experience its pleasures and rewards.

There is growing evidence that altruism is associated with fewer psychological problems and greater subjective well-being, a person's emotional and cognitive sense of the quality of his or her life. Whether there is a causal relationship, whether altruism leads to better mental health, is a more complicated question. Some research suggests that it does, provided it is done in manageable doses. Feeling overwhelmed by other people's questions and demands is not very healthy. Too much is too much.

Altruism and happiness

Although popular belief states that you become happy by paying more attention to and spending more time on yourself, research suggests the opposite: altruistic behavior can make you happier.

This seems to be the case at an early age. One study found that toddlers under the age of two were happier when they gave candy to a doll than when they were given candy themselves. They were even happier when they gave candy from their own candy box. Other studies found that spending money on other people was associated with a significantly greater sense of happiness, regardless of income level, while this was not the case for spending money on oneself. This suggests that changing our behavior patterns by giving a few dollars a month can make us significantly happier. In many people, a positive interaction occurs between altruism and happiness: contributing to someone else's happiness makes them happy, which may encourage them to do so again.

Most of the above studies that have examined the link between giving and happiness were done with participants from WEIRD countries (Western, Educated, Industrialized, Rich, and Democratic countries). This raises the question of whether this link is a universal or rather a cultural phenomenon. A study was designed with people from 136 countries to answer this question. The survey data showed that people who had been charitable in the past year reported a greater sense of happiness, regardless of possible influencing factors such as family income, age, gender, marital status, education, and even possible food shortages.

A second part of the study asked people from three countries—Canada, Uganda, and India—to recall a time when they had spent money on themselves or someone else. Across the three countries, participants who had to remember spending money on someone else reported feeling better than those who had to remember spending money on themselves. This effect appeared to be independent of whether the money was spent on a stranger or on a friend (to promote social relationships which could lead to greater happiness).

In a third part of the study, Canadian and South African participants were given the option of anonymously purchasing a bag of candy. Half of them were told they would buy the treats for themselves. The other half were told they would buy it for a sick child they would never meet. In both cultures, the participants who bought the candy for the sick child reported a greater positive effect than those who bought it for themselves. This suggests that people still experience more happiness from giving to others they will never meet than from spending on themselves. So, the link between altruism and happiness seems to be universal.

People who are focused too hard on themselves never have enough. They always experience a deficit and are constantly worried about what they don't have or what they might lose. That's partly why they don't give. But people who have learned to be generous know that their own lives are positively affected in several ways by sharing with others. Altruistic behavior causally leads to a greater sense of happiness, better health, emotional well-being, and a sense of purpose in life. It is thus "paid back", which helps explain its perpetuation.

It is hard to find a generous person who is cranky and unhappy. People willing to share their time, possessions, and talents are often among the happiest people around. We are all looking for some meaning in our existence, the feeling that we are contributing something. Altruistic people are happier giving than receiving.

HEALTHY ALTRUISM

The word "selfish" feels like a swear word, an adjective with a decidedly negative connotation. We seem to want to prove that we are not selfish. We volunteer for the school committee, we spend sleepless nights sewing costumes for the school play, and we offer a listening ear and a shoulder to cry on. Beware, it's a slippery slope from the heroic "I'll take care of it!" to the martyrdom "Why do I always have to do everything around here!?"

Selfishness and altruism are almost always presented as opposites. In doing so, selfishness is viewed as bad, an undesirable, or even an immoral trait with negative consequences for others, while altruism is usually viewed as good, as desirable, and virtuous with only positive consequences. The reality, however, is more complex: not all forms of selfishness are necessarily bad, and not all forms of altruism are necessarily good, even with the best of intentions.

People possess two systems: an "ego-system" motivated by a desire for positive impressions of others, and an "eco-system" motivated by promoting the well-being of others.

People motivated by their "ego-system" may sometimes engage in altruistic behavior, not because they genuinely care about the welfare of others and want to be constructive and supportive, but as a conscious or unconscious strategy to influence the opinion of others.

Healthy selfishness

The cultural taboo on selfishness leads some people to feel guilty about exhibiting healthy self-love, when respect for one's own happiness, one's own growth and one's own freedom are very important for mental balance. The form of selfishness that is condemned by society—an interest only in oneself and an inability to guarantee the dignity and integrity of others with pleasure and respect—is the opposite of self-love. It is a type of greed, a bottomless pit that exhausts the person in an endless attempt to satisfy a need that will never be satisfied. Maslow advocated the need to distinguish between "healthy" and "unhealthy" selfishness, between healthy and unhealthy motivations for one's seemingly selfish behavior.

Studies have shown that people with a healthy form of selfishness take better care of themselves and are not paralyzed by an overdose of empathy for the problems of others. They typically feel better about themselves, have more positive relationships, are more assertive, and have an easier time helping others. Such individuals experience pleasure in helping others. Some forms of selfish behavior may be good or even necessary at certain times, and bad at others. Just as selfless behavior is sometimes good and at other times can be bad.

Unhealthy altruism

Research on altruism has almost always focused on the positive aspects of altruism, how people are naturally configured to care for the well-being of others and reduce their suffering. Western societies have become so focused on the benefits that the downside has been almost completely ignored.

Altruism becomes unhealthy when a person feels the (sometimes pathological) need to sacrifice themselves for the good of others, when the mental obligation arises to always do more and more. This can lead to excessive and potentially harmful behavior or even depression or burnout. Unhealthy (or pathological) altruists irrationally place the needs of another above their own, in a way that causes harm to themselves. The main underlying motivation for these types of altruists is to please others, gain admiration and approval, and avoid criticism and rejection. Unhealthy altruists lack healthy selfishness. Their altruistic behavior is then a kind of façade behind which they hide in their search for appreciation. However, when that appreciation does not come, behind that façade often arises anger, frustration, and resentment because they have to sacrifice so much and get so little in return.

"Healthy" altruism

We thus find ourselves with a double paradox. On the one hand, healthy egoism seems to be related to various aspects of altruism. On the other hand, unhealthy altruism seems to be linked to a certain selfish motivation.

We believe in "healthy" altruism: behavior activated by the "eco-system" to promote the true well-being of others, without sacrificing our own well-being. This kind of sacrifice is not sustainable over time and thus ultimately not good, neither for ourselves nor for the people we want to help.

People who exhibit "healthy" altruistic behavior voluntarily decide when to help others and contribute to the well-being of others because they want to, not because they feel obligated to. They do this because they feel it is the right thing to do, not because of what others think about it. They do this to become a better person in their own eyes, not through the eyes of others. They do what they want to do and give what they want to give. "Healthy" altruists protect their fuel tanks and see it as their responsibility to put the lid on and off in time without draining it.

ALTRUISM IN TIMES OF COVID-19

Throughout history, major crises have given rise to great expressions of solidarity. Just think of the famine in Ethiopia in 1985, the earthquake in Armenia in 1989, the genocide in Rwanda in 1994, the Indonesian tsunami in 2004, or the earthquake that devastated Haiti in 2010. Thus, in the short term, altruists can be expected to step up and focus their contributions on health, clinical and basic research, or vulnerable populations hit the hardest by the COVID-19 crisis.

The question, however, is whether this altruistic behavior will be sustained in a long-distance race. The health crisis we are experiencing is global and accompanied by an unprecedented economic crisis. This will inevitably have consequences. How will small and medium-sized donors react when their jobs, their businesses, or even their relationships come under pressure? How will large donors react when their markets collapse and their return on investment is close to zero?

The Charities Aid Foundation's 2021 World Giving Index pandemic report provides part of the answer. In the report, we see big differences from the results of the past decade. Countries like the United States, the United Kingdom, Canada, and the Netherlands disappeared from the top 10, and Nigeria, Ghana, Uganda, and Kosovo took their place. Belgium and France even dropped from places 42 and 66 respectively to 112 and 106. This makes Belgium the third last on the list! The pandemic seems to have had a very clear impact on altruistic behavior: mutual solidarity in the so-called "rich" countries has declined significantly during the crisis, while we see just the opposite movement in the "poor" countries. We should note though, that the severe lockdowns in Western countries may have made it more difficult for many people to help strangers or to engage in volunteering activities. The key question now is whether these findings will be confirmed and whether this trend will continue in the coming years.

Alongside this observation, we are seeing behaviors we have never witnessed before—some deeply moving, others relentless. When disaster strikes, the media easily creates the impression that we are all selfish. Reports of panic buying, fights over toilet paper, and profiteering are examples, as are stories of the callous dismissal of long-serving staff. But many more stories need to be told. Stories of communities joining hands, of young and healthy people running errands for the elderly, of cooks cooking for overworked hospital staff, and of musicians playing concerts on their balconies to keep the spirit of people in quarantine up. Many companies support frontline medical personnel by offering their products or premises for free or by switching to producing items that are desperately needed. Many small and not-so-small acts of altruism take place all over the world.

During a pandemic like this one, altruism is more important than ever. Not only is it a powerful tool to keep up the spirits, but it is also necessary to beat the virus. We cannot stop the coronavirus unless we realize we are all connected. Our actions have serious consequences for others and carry ethical weight—including how much food and toilet paper we buy, how often we go out, and how much physical distance we keep from others. Remarkably, certain cultures—such as China and South Korea—have handled the outbreak more effectively than those countries where individualism, economic considerations, and personal freedoms are held in higher regard than the welfare of the collective.

"*What is not good for the hive is not good for the bee.*" The words of Emperor Marcus Aurelius are searingly current. The Roman philosopher Seneca gave another wonderful picture of our interconnectedness: "*Our mutual relations are like an arch of stone that would collapse if the stones did not mutually support each other.*" When the foundation of our civilization is in danger, every little stone matters. We must think about the arch and our place in it. Ultimately, it is also in our own best interest. We must remember that we are in this together, abandon selfishness, and help those who need our help the most. Generosity and altruism will help us get through the current pandemic with intact minds. It is what will bring us closer together and strengthen the collective. A world without altruism is like an engine without lubricant—it would soon overheat and shut down. Without altruism, our society collapses.

Charities Aid Foundation
2021 CAF World Giving Index
Pandemic Special Report

ALTRUISM IN SUMMARY

· Compassion and empathy are feelings that give rise to generous and altruistic behavior.

· Helping to solve others' problems is more important than the debate over pure versus impure altruism.

· Although, like most animal species, we are genetically programmed to cooperate, anonymously helping people we do not know is a unique trait of humans.

· Altruistic behavior is innate but must be stimulated and maintained if we don't want to lose it.

· There are significant differences in the way people from different cultures see the world. It is wrong to think that our Western view is the only correct one.

· Altruism and generosity are not limited to people from richer countries but take place all over the world.

· The religious, social, and cultural context in which a person lives all impact a person's altruistic behavior.

- A combination of intrinsic and extrinsic motivators influences altruistic behavior.

- Studies have shown a positive relationship between altruism, health, and happiness.

- Healthy selfishness and healthy altruism can go perfectly well together; unhealthy selfishness and unhealthy altruism have pernicious consequences for everyone.

- Altruism is essential for our society to withstand and overcome a crisis like the COVID-19 pandemic.

Action

"*The difference between what we do and what we are capable of doing would suffice to solve most of the world's problems.*"

—Mahatma Gandhi

COMMON
THINKING
MISTAKES

Why does one person go get groceries for an elderly neighbor and another mainly stocks up his own cart? Why does someone turn his head away from the problems of others? Why do some give some change to the man or woman at the traffic light every day? We all have a natural predisposition for altruism, but between us, there are differences in DNA, upbringing, and other environmental factors. If you grow up in a culture where distrust prevails, you learn to have little trust in others yourself.

Healthy altruism makes our world a better place. It improves the life of the receiver and the giver as well as the society in which both live. The great thing is that anyone can exhibit altruistic behavior, regardless of their position in life, how much they have, or what they hope to have someday. We are one hundred percent convinced that deep in our hearts, we all want to help a child in need. We would immediately invite a hungry child to our table without giving it much thought. We would give it books or shoes to go to school without questioning it. And yet we don't.

The plight of the poor induces unease and guilt in many of us, so we build cognitive buffers to protect ourselves from these uncomfortable emotions. These barriers present themselves as rational arguments that prevent us from taking action. This does not mean that we are indifferent to the suffering of others, but that we handle our empathy poorly. To turn our empathy into action, it is important to recognize and correct our cognitive and emotional thinking errors.

Mistake #1: Fatality

"That's the way it is, it will never change anyway."

There has always been hunger in the world, and there always will be. Some things will never change. We sometimes believe that the fate of people or countries is fixed and cannot be changed. Although change can be slow, making it seem like nothing changes, things evolve! Can you imagine Catholic Poland will ever be as open on topics like sex and abortion as Sweden, one of the most liberal countries in the world? And yet, in 1960, abortion was illegal in Sweden and young pregnant Swedish college students traveled to Poland to have abortions. Five years later, Poland banned abortion, and Sweden legalized it. Things change.

Today, North Korea and Venezuela are two of the worst countries to live in, while South Korea and Chile are highly developed, rich, and fairly democratic nations. It is tempting to argue that capitalism and democracy bring peace and prosperity while communism stands for damnation. Had you visited these four countries in the 1970s, you would think differently; back then, Venezuela was so rich it was called Saudi Venezuela, and people in North Korea earned more than their southern neighbors. Besides, South Korea and Chile were ruled by military dictatorships.

Countries, societies, cultures, and religions are constantly evolving. Some knowledge ages quickly. What was true 10 or 20 years ago is not necessarily so today. Thanks to technological advances, some things that took years in the past sometimes happen in just a few months today. Talk to your parents and grandparents if you are still not convinced. They will remind you how some values and life have changed.

Mistake #2: Magnitude

"The problem is so big that my help won't make a difference anyway." "There are so many good causes. I don't know where to start."

This attitude states that the magnitude of problems in impoverished societies is so enormous, complex, and hopeless that no solution is possible, making help pointless. It depends on your perspective. If you look at your contribution in isolation, you are probably right. You will not solve the overall problem. However, the underlying thinking is murky: if I can't solve the total problem, I better do nothing.

Imagine you go to a doctor for a suspicious lump on your neck. The doctor performs a biopsy and confirms that you have cancer, but refuses to treat you. He claims that, in the richest countries alone, over 1 million people a year die from cancer. The disease is epidemic and therefore cannot be adequately addressed. He cannot cure everyone, so good luck and goodbye. Would this be rational? Can anyone imagine visiting a doctor who refuses treatment until he can also cure all his other patients?

This kind of attitude is based on the all-or-nothing fallacy. It claims that if you cannot help all the people, there is no point in helping any of them. Curiously, this reasoning is never used in prosperous countries. Requests for dental, medical, and psychological care, financial counseling, education, and so on are never rejected because not everyone can be helped and as a result, no one will be helped.

Sometimes we think we should only give something substantial. That if we can't give 50 or 100 euros, we better not give anything at all because we would be labeled as stingy. However, many little ones make a big one and even if your contribution is just a small drop in the ocean, it can make quite a difference where it falls. Some achievements require only a few drops. For example, it is relatively easy to work with a few friends, family, or colleagues to fund a soup kitchen in an area where people live in extreme poverty. This can easily provide a daily hot meal to 50 to 100 people. This has a direct impact on their health, allowing them to work, earn an income and outgrow their extreme poverty situation. Who said you couldn't make a difference?

Don't let your empathy paralyze you. You can't always respond positively to every request for support. Don't feel bad because you can't help everyone, but feel good because you can help someone. Think about your affinities, about what is closest to your heart. Research, prioritize and make choices. Maybe go for one or two major goals and consider a smaller support for a few others. Remember that some people have to live on less than $2 a day?

Mistake #3: Social distance

"There are heaps of people at home who need help."

A third fallacy involves thinking that we should first help those in need in our own circle, family, or community before we look beyond our borders. Charity should be focused on our own country, where we have our own needs and greater obligations. This attitude does not question the usefulness of helping the Third World, but gives it a lower priority than our local needs.

This attitude is a protest that argues that sending money abroad is insensitive, or even offensive because it ignores our local problems. It would ignore how hard life is in our own country. This objection is well-founded: for many people in developed countries, life is hard. But if we recognize how hard it is here, how much harder must it be without education, food, clean water, medical care, or adequate housing? How much harder can it be to live on $2 a day?

Of course, local charity should not be discouraged. Fortunately, one does not have to exclude the other. It is a normal instinct to take care of yourself, your family, and your loved ones. It is human to be more generous or to sacrifice more for the good of people you know than for people you don't, and there is nothing wrong with that. Don't feel guilty because you are in a position where it is a little harder to help others. But don't forget to put things in their proper perspective, even in tough times. What does "tough" mean? Not being able to go on vacation this year? Having to put off buying a new car? Or not being able to go to the doctor? Not knowing if your children will have anything to eat the next day?

This fallacy of equating extreme poverty with poverty at home alleviates our responsibility and the accompanying guilt evoked by our empathy. It allows us to focus more on our concerns than on the problems of others, as they would be of relatively equal magnitude, and our first obligation would be to ourselves.

Mistake #4: Law of nature

"Poverty is a natural fact."

This attitude states that the earth regulates itself and that populations must learn to live and reproduce within the limits of available natural resources. Poverty is said to arise because the environment cannot sustain human life at a given population size. Insufficient food and clean water are a natural consequence of too many people in relation to the available resources. The solution then would be to limit the number of people in a given geographic area. Nature does this by creating famine. Intervening in this natural mechanism would further upset the balance and cause an even greater catastrophe once the relief effort can no longer be sustained. This kind of reasoning is absurd.

During the global financial crisis and high unemployment of the past decade, no one suggested that unemployed people in richer countries should disappear so that the balance between workers and jobs would be restored. No one argues that overpopulation causes unemployment, although a significant reduction in population could certainly have improved the crisis. Everyone agrees that a host of variables related to inadequate regulation and risky financial practices caused the crisis. A confluence of events not unlike periods of hunger and famine abroad caused by political corruption and wars. Why do thoughtful, compassionate, and intelligent people in affluent countries regard unemployment as a crisis, and accept the deaths of 15,000 young children a day because of extreme poverty?

By linking the fate of the extremely poor to the laws of nature against which we cannot and should not intervene, we eliminate our responsibility and again reduce our feelings of guilt and concern caused by our empathy. However, this attitude ignores the fact that no individual can do anything to prevent being born into extreme poverty. No one has control over where he or she is born, a twist of fate that is the most decisive factor in the course of our lives.

Mistake #5: Responsibility

"Each country is responsible for solving its own problems."

This attitude states that it is the responsibility of the people in the poorest countries to solve their own problems, and that wealthy individuals in richer countries are under no obligation to provide them with help. This relies on the question of who is responsible for the problems of society. Is it only the members of that society, according to national or ethnic boundaries, or does responsibility extend beyond those boundaries?

Responsibility for one's actions is a powerful philosophy with impressive results. But it assumes people have the skills and resources to make something of their lives and that is where the shoe pinches. It is precisely this context (skills and resources) that is absent in societies where extreme poverty prevails. The extremely poor have been deprived of this context for generations. How many people, anywhere, can build a successful life on $2 a day without potable water, medical care, schooling, or sufficient food? Suppose the father who lives next door to you regularly beats and terrorizes his children. According to the above logic, no one would have the responsibility to intervene and help the children, because it is the family's responsibility to solve its own problems. Most of us, of course, would object and argue that the children are powerless victims. To do nothing would be criminal. In what way is this moral logic different for children living in extreme poverty? No extenuating circumstance can stand up to the screams of the terrorized children at the neighbors. The cries of distress from the extremely poor children are no different. We just hear them less because they come from further away.

Even if one were to argue that adults can live decent lives in conditions of extreme poverty, how can one deny the suffering of children? Do their parents (if they still have them) bear the blame? Does this argument seem plausible for the terrorized children of neighbors?

Mistake #6: Trust

"My contribution will not be spent on the right things."

They won't spend my support on the right things, or worse, they might waste it. I would use it differently. That's not what I would have done. We think we know better, so we choose not to give. Altruism always requires a certain amount of trust. To give away our resources, we must believe that people will use them wisely. This applies to charitable organizations and to individuals or communities in need of help.

Larger charitable organizations are businesses that need to cover their costs. They often employ people, do marketing campaigns to raise funds, and so on. Some costs they incur are investments to optimize their operations. Transparency has increased in the last decade. You can find much information and evidence on the Internet. If a charitable organization wants to be officially recognized (and issue tax certificates, for example), they are also audited regularly to make sure that the funds they receive are used for the right purposes. It is always a good idea to check the operating costs of the organizations you support.

In recent years, several initiatives have emerged that offer direct help (through direct cash transfers) to extremely poor people, without conditions and advice. The first results are already encouraging. Trust works, since most people "just" have good intentions and work hard to improve their living conditions. It works better than charity structures that start from a "distrustful, wait-and-see" attitude. As a caregiver, you may feel valuable, but sadly, that's where most of it stops. Giving people the opportunities to make their own choices works better than taking the initiative out of their hands. It is more efficient, realistic, and humane. It is rarely a good idea to impose certain initiatives without being supported by the people in question. It only leads to reinforcing a sense of inferiority, wrong decisions, and frustration on both sides.

Instead of using such defensive cognitive distortions as an excuse not to help, we should rather embrace our empathy. This carries risks, but creates tremendous opportunities and offers countless benefits. Empathy is the basis for love, cooperation, and altruism. Often, exposure to situations in which extremely poor people live leads to greater understanding and connection. This is exactly our experience. We did not plan our commitment, but, once exposed to the poor, we made it our mission to assist them. Instead of fearing our empathy and defending ourselves against our guilt, we turned it into positive energy that has improved and continues to improve countless lives. What more could we wish for?

THE POVERTY
CYCLE

Living in extreme poverty means not being able to afford a doctor or medical treatment. It means no electricity, limited shelter, and often little to no food on the table. For young children, inadequate nutrition leads to growth retardation with lasting effects on their development. In regions where many people lack access to clean water and sanitation, extreme poverty means the spread of disease and unnecessary child mortality.

Children living in poverty rarely have access to quality education. Sometimes this is because there are not enough quality schools, because their parents cannot afford the cost, or because impoverished families need their children to work. Without a quality education, children grow up unable to cater to their own children—thus, poverty is passed from generation to generation. The situation is usually compounded by a lack of self-confidence, a sense of inferiority, and sometimes even the belief that living in such conditions is their fate, about which they cannot do anything.

Economists use the term "poverty trap" to describe a situation in which people are stuck in deprivation for long periods, often several generations, and they can do nothing to escape this situation. The idea is simple: poverty today causes poverty in the future, so children born into poverty remain poor. For a person to get out of poverty, they need opportunities such as education, clean water, financial resources, and accessible medical facilities. Without these basic elements, poverty becomes a cycle from one generation to the next, in a perpetual motion.

If families are too poor to send their children to school, their children will have a hard time earning an adequate income later. If a community has no clean water, women will spend much of their day fetching water rather than earning an income. If medical facilities are far away, a parent will lose income every time he takes a sick child to the doctor.

Natural disasters and conflict make it even harder to break this vicious cycle and often plunge additional people into the poverty trap. Families in a community without well-functioning public institutions usually have few reserves, so when such catastrophes occur, they become further entrenched in poverty or fall into a precarious situation quickly.

Malnutrition is one of the typical causes that can drive people into a poverty trap. When our bodies use the calories we consume to survive rather than to provide the necessary strength to work, a perverse equilibrium is created characterized by low income and poor nutrition.

Inadequate nutrition then becomes both the cause and the consequence of low income.

Such vicious circles also occur at a macro level. For example, low-income countries often lack basic conditions for growth (such as technology, education, and infrastructure). These are much needed to achieve productivity improvements that lead to rising national incomes, which would eventually allow the population to escape the most extreme forms of poverty.

To make the right decisions to "break the cycle", it is important to understand the poverty trap in which an individual, a family, or a community finds itself. Onetime efforts, if well-chosen, can have lasting positive effects. This is the reasoning used, for example, to advocate to expand the micro-finance system in low-income countries. Often, someone simply lacks a push to start a virtuous cycle of increased investment, economic growth, and income.

One specific trigger, such as malnutrition or disease, rarely causes a poverty trap. It is usually a complex situation with multiple causes that will require a multidimensional approach. This does not always have to be done at a regional or national level. Sometimes the chances of success are just as high or even higher, with measures aimed at addressing bottlenecks at a local or even family level.

WHERE TO START?

Although correlation does not mean causation, there is a clear link between poverty and health, education, and, to a slightly lesser extent, the protection of human rights.

Poverty and health

Newborn life expectancy is the most widely used measure to describe the health status of a population. The good news is that historical data shows that global life expectancy has increased dramatically over the past few decades, with significant long-term improvements in all countries of the world. The recent increase in life expectancy in most developing countries has been nothing short of spectacular.

Despite this positive evolution, there are huge disparities still to be addressed: in several countries in Sub-Saharan Africa, the average life expectancy is still less than 60 years, compared to over 80 years in countries in Europe or Japan.

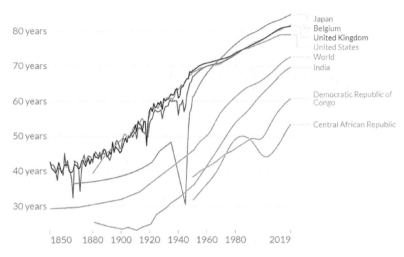

Figure 21: Evolution of life expectancy (1850-2015)
(Source: ourworldindata.org/life-expectancy)

Drastic reductions in child and maternal mortality have been critical to improving life expectancy around the world. In less than three decades, child mortality has more than halved—from 12.6 million in 1990 to 5.4 million in 2017. Child mortality has never been lower. Of course, the death of any child is an enormous tragedy, and in many countries, too many children still die from causes we can prevent and treat. In Sub-Saharan Africa, there are still countries with infant mortality rates above 10%—this means that one in 10 children never reaches their fifth birthday. Inequality remains huge: in low-income countries, child mortality rates are on average more than 10 times higher than in high-income countries.

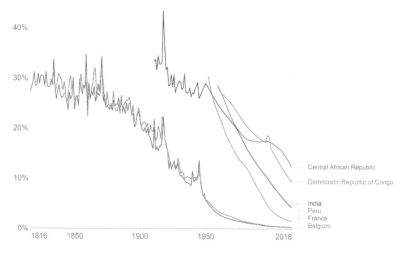

Figure 22: Evolution of infant mortality (1800-2016)
(Source: ourworldindata.org/child-mortality)

Although the general health situation worldwide has improved considerably, it remains problematic in the poorest regions and vulnerable areas. The solutions are often known and available but do not reach the people who need them. This is even the case in countries where most health indicators are green (before the outbreak of the COVID-19 crisis). During our conversation with Patricia Garcia, former Minister of Health in Peru from July 2016 to September 2017, this was very clear. According to her, most of the poor do not know their rights to health care, and local medical aid stations too often stockpile medicines for future needs instead of administering them to people who need them now.

Poverty and education

Education is widely regarded as a fundamental building block, both for individuals and for societies. In most countries today, basic education is not only a right but also a duty—governments are expected to ensure access to basic education, while citizens are often legally required to receive education up to a certain basic level. Literacy rates have increased worldwide over the last two centuries, mainly because of an increase in elementary school enrollment. Secondary and higher education have also experienced spectacular growth, with the average number of years children attend school worldwide now being much higher than 20 or 30 years ago. Despite this, some countries have fallen behind, again, especially in Sub-Saharan Africa, where there are still countries with literacy rates below 50%.

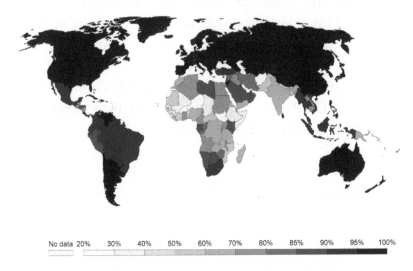

No data 20%   30%   40%   50%   60%   70%   80%   85%   90%   95%   100%

Figure 23: Overview of global literacy rates (2011)
(Source: CIA Factbook via ourworldindata.org/global-rise-of-education)

Literacy rate data by age group show that there is a large generational gap in almost all developing countries: younger generations are progressively better educated than their predecessors. This suggests that in these countries, literacy rates for the total population will continue to increase. According to a forecast by the International Institute for Applied Systems Analysis (IIASA), by 2050, only five countries are likely to have an adult illiteracy rate of over 20%: Burkina Faso, Ethiopia, Guinea, Mali, and Niger.

Enrollment and attendance rates are two important measures for understanding a country's access to education. Elementary school enrollment rates are usually calculated from administrative data in official records. Attendance rates are mostly measured using data from family surveys.

In most developing countries, the enrollment rate is considerably higher than the attendance rate. Many children who are admittedly enrolled do not attend school regularly. Low attendance rates are a significant problem in sub-Saharan Africa. For example, in Niger, Chad, and Liberia, it is estimated that less than half of school-age children attend elementary school. They must work to help the family meet their basic needs and take care of their younger siblings, or they cannot afford shoes or a uniform, making them the target of ridicule from their more affluent age-mates.

Poverty and human rights

Human rights describe the moral norms, values, and standards that are fundamental rights of every human being. They include the right to a fair trial, protection of physical integrity, protection from slavery, the right to freedom of expression, and the right to education. The protection of human rights is one of the most important aspects of development. Yet it receives far less attention than health and education, partly because it is more difficult to measure and partly because it is outside the sphere of NGOs.

More affluent countries protect the human rights of their populations better than poorer countries, although a few countries are exceptions (e.g., Saudi Arabia concerning women and Israel concerning Palestinian minorities).

These averages are good indicators, but they only give a partial picture of the reality that people living in extreme poverty face daily. Usually, there are several factors at play which are intertwined and mutually reinforcing. While this can complicate possible solution scenarios—a problem caused by one cause is easier to address than one caused by multiple factors—, working on one aspect usually has beneficial effects on the other related causes. For example, malaria control improves health, allowing children to attend school, which ultimately increases their chances of escaping extreme poverty.

While the contexts in which families and communities live in extreme poverty can be very different, a focus on health and education is usually a good starting point. Initiatives that focus on these strengthen the basic conditions needed for these groups to have a real chance of outgrowing their situation and breaking the vicious cycle of extreme poverty.

THE HEAD AND
THE HEART

Suppose you meet a child on the street who is dying of hunger and you have a loaf of bread with you. It would be immoral to walk on and eat the bread yourself. Worldwide, thousands of children die of hunger. Because they happen not to live on our street, it is no less immoral to ignore them. Suppose you have no bread, but a dollar (and many more dollars in your bank account). Do you then give it so the hungry child can buy food? Of course. But then it is inconsistent for you to keep that dollar and not give it away for children on another continent.

If we approach altruism purely rationally, we need to optimize both our contribution (how much we give) and our impact (return). How can I give as much as I can? Can I earn more by taking a different job, which allows me to give more away? That's what some people do. How do I get the greatest return on what I give? For that, I need evidence.

The "Effective Altruism" movement applies capitalist principles to achieve social goals. According to Peter Singer, one founder of this philosophy and author of the thought experiment above, capitalism and altruism can be perfectly compatible. Effective Altruism does not imply ignoring compassion. On the contrary, "it is precisely the reason we do not want to be satisfied with doing good, but want to do as much good as possible." This is nothing new. After all, most religious traditions consider it a duty for the believer to give to those who are poorer. And the welfare state in our democratic societies devotes much of its budget to redistributing a minimum income to the least well-off.

Singer prefers reason to emotion, the head to the heart. If we want to reduce suffering in this world as much as possible, we must ensure that our gifts generate as many positive effects as possible. Instead of easing our conscience by simply doing something, we must look at the consequences, at how our donation is used.

In his book "The most good you can do", Peter Singer illustrates his reasoning with many examples and testimonials from students or strangers whose choices are unusual. Some voluntarily give up a career (e.g., teaching philosophy) for a much more rewarding profession that allows them to give more (e.g., financial trader on Wall Street). This altruism prompts some to go even further. Zell Kravinsky donated a kidney to a stranger. He justifies his choice by saying that the risk of dying, in this case, is 1 in 4,000. "Not giving a kidney to someone who needs it is like thinking our life is worth 4,000 times more than a stranger's," he explains. Effective altruists talk "about how many people they can help," more than about how much they can help a person.

A priori, it seems more obvious to help a poor person who lives down the street from us rather than strangers on the African continent. The former has a face. You can start a conversation with him or her, and you can directly hand him or her some money. Singer does not deny this, but he argues that this does not make the best use of resources. His approach is based on utilitarianism, an emancipatory, liberal-inspired movement that holds as a moral principle of action that the greatest good should be done for the greatest number or that the suffering of the greatest number should be reduced. This would technically mean that you should not hesitate to push your loved one in front of a train if doing so could save the lives of five innocent victims tied up on the tracks. Utilitarianism rejects anything that is not based on rational arguments but on feelings, emotions, or principles often inspired by religion. Anyone attempting to save human lives or make people's lives more pleasant must make hard choices.

William MacAskill, another founder of the "Effective Altruism" movement, illustrates this through the story of James Orbinski, a Canadian physician and former director of Doctors Without Borders. In the mid-1990s, he worked in a small Red Cross hospital in Rwanda. He found himself in the middle of the flaring violence between the Hutus and the Tutsis. The many victims who came into Orbinski's hospital presented him with tough choices. His team could not cope with the number of wounded. To apply method, each victim was given a number: one meant "treat immediately," two stood for "provide medical help within 24 hours," and three meant "cannot be saved". A gruesome situation, which forced Orbinski to choose how to spend his limited resources so that as many lives as possible were saved. Helping means choosing. Those who give a portion of their income to the AIDS Fund prefer to fight HIV over fighting other life-threatening diseases. Those who spend a year volunteering in South America have decided not to give their time to people in Bangladesh. According to the Effective Altruism philosophy, the choice should be based on the number of lives that can be saved.

Consider how many people will benefit from your gift, and to what extent they will be helped. Ask yourself if this is the most effective thing you can do. See if your chosen cause is not already supported by thousands of others. Reason: what will happen if I make a different choice? And finally, ask yourself what the chances of success are and how great that success will be. Those who consistently ask themselves these questions when they do something for others can call themselves effective altruists, according to MacAskill.

The parallels between this "altruistic" approach and the investor seeking the highest return on his or her investment may feel counterintuitive and come as a shock to some. Yet this radical philosophy appeals to a lot of millennials, as well as Bill Gates or Warren Buffett, who spend billions of dollars fighting poverty and misery in Africa through foundations.

Altruism, however, is not a purely scientific fact, and approaching it this way falls short of the interests, passions, and emotions of the giver. A human being does not live purely rationally, weighing up costs and benefits each time.

We buy a piece of cake because we like it without asking ourselves whether it wouldn't have been better to buy something else with those pennies. Let alone whether it wouldn't be better to give the money away to someone who can't afford a piece of cake. We do not explicitly consider how purposefully we spend our money, not in a supermarket, while traveling, with friends, or for ourselves. We make choices that meet our most important needs and that we feel best about.

Why should this be different for our altruistic behavior? Should we approach our philanthropy clinically and decide as a business manager who makes investments according to expected returns? If we want to be consistent with this logic, we better not fund a guide dog that will help one blind person in our own country. Rather, we should spend this money on purchasing medicines that can treat trachoma (an inflammation that can cause blindness) in a thousand people in a developing country. Investing in solutions that make the lives of people with disabilities more bearable is not a good option either. For the same money, we better buy a few thousand mosquito nets to protect children from malaria. And how do we justify the new bicycle for our offspring when a few thousand kilometers away, children are starving to death? Such a rational way of thinking and living is certainly fodder for an interesting ethical discussion, but it will not win you many friends in your immediate environment.

Fortunately, altruism does not need to be a dilemma between two extremes. As philosopher John Gray notes, "We can choose between spending time relieving the suffering of a dying person or working to donate the money earned to an effective charity. There is no right answer." We can decide for ourselves how much money we are willing to spend on charities, and how much we reserve for our own families. We can decide how much to donate to dementia research, to supporting the homeless, to fighting parasite worm infections in children, and to sheltering stray cats. But in each category, we must choose whether we prefer to support a cause for which we have a subjective preference or one that maximizes world welfare.

Is it better to reach as many people as possible or to help a community, a family, or an individual as best you can? Do you better focus on one priority or commit to several goals? Do you go for a business "Return on Investment" approach and spend your time, energy, and money in such a way that it yields the highest potential return? Or do you rely more on your feelings and emotions and do you prefer to support a cause that is close to your heart? Do you follow your head or your heart?

People have personal, complex, and irrational motivations to do good. Making the eventual choice purely dependent on arithmetic and abstract models, while an interesting train of thought and a touchstone for your own motives and preferences, is a bridge too far for many. Altruism is not driven solely by reason or emotion, but by both. Not by the head or the heart, but by the head and the heart. Everyone should try to find a balance between quantifiable impact and subjective personal valuations. This is the best way to be effective. The impact on the receiver's side is significant, and the giver sees evidence of results in those areas close to his heart, putting him in a positive altruistic spiral.

Peter Singer
The why and how of Effective Altruism
TED Talk

THE WHITE
SAVIOR COMPLEX

The term "white savior complex" refers to a white person acting to help non-whites, but in a context that can be construed as selfish. The white person is represented as the benefactor who comes to the rescue of the poor, usually persons of color. This kind of representation is problematic because it reinforces the idea that Africa and other poor parts of the world are vast and hopeless deserts of poverty, a representation that is not at all consistent with reality. It creates a one-sided image of the people and their living conditions. It usually arises unconsciously and results from an admittedly well-intentioned action that may ultimately prove counterproductive.

The white savior complex manifests itself in several ways. As Western people, we readily assume that we know what is good for someone in a problem situation—even for someone we meet on the street in a country and culture that is not our own. We know what is best for them and therefore what the solution is. We take action without thinking about the possible consequences. An Irish family, while touring Peru, visited a slum in Lima. They were struck by the situation of a single mother living with her four young children in a rickety cardboard shack. They took action and financed the construction of a wooden house. It seemed like a wonderful act of altruism. However, in poor areas, families often survive thanks to community solidarity. The balance there is fragile and can easily be disturbed, with serious consequences. Community members began to ignore the family, stopped coming to see if everything was okay, and stopped sharing leftovers because "they were being helped anyway." The situation worsened day by day and eventually, the family had to leave the community.

Volunteers who go on missions to help children usually do so with the belief that these children are living in hardship and that they will help to improve their lives or solve their problems. They come for a limited period with the promise of giving children hope for a better future. The reality, however, is that they are part of a rotating cast of characters who enter the lives of these children, try to connect with them for a short while, and leave again at the end of their volunteer period. They "sample" the culture and daily life of these children; then they pack their suitcases and leave the children back to their own devices. They sometimes cause more psychological damage to the children and communities they visit than if they had never come.

Charity collections are often used to dump old, unnecessary, or unusable items. Is this what they need or is this what we want to get rid of? Aid organizations usually receive more things they don't need than things they have asked for. This leads to more work for the organizations, both in their search for what they really need and in sorting and disposing of what they cannot use. The assumption that "these people will be satisfied with everything" is misleading and arrogant. If you would be offended if someone donated it to you, don't give it.

People in need are often voiceless, not because they have no voice, but because they have no opportunity to make their voice heard. We often praise the many personalities who use their platform to bring attention to various issues, but we rarely see them offer their platform to those who have relevant experiences or an authentic story. Instead of speaking on behalf of marginalized groups, they would do better to let them guide by those who need help. Many are not helpless and know what to do about their situation. They just need an audience to listen and a platform to present, empower and find support for their solutions.

Everyone knows the typical cliché pictures of Western "rescuers" with a poor baby in their arms, the leading hero, and the suffering secondary figure. It places the rescuer at the center of the situation and shifts the conversation to how he is "such a good person" rather than emphasizing the actual need. In addition, it perpetuates an image that all babies of color depend on white or Western help to feel safe and comfortable. Imagine that together we get on a plane and fly to Stockholm or London. Upon arrival, we all encounter cute little children—other people's children—whom we lift and take selfies with that we then post on Facebook. Sounds strange, right?

We too, have made similar mistakes. We have taken what we thought were cool, cultural pictures of people in their

everyday lives, without permission. We have become im-
patient with the work pace of certain cultures, mistakenly
assuming that our Western work ethic is the most efficient.
We have over-simplified people and cultures by outlining a
"poor but happy" narrative. We have over-exalted customs
and characteristics of other cultures in a way that makes
them exotic.

Such behavior leads to an attitude of superiority over, or
depending on the angle, a sense of inferiority among those
who "need help." It is counterproductive, patronizing, and
leads to paternalism. It presents us as heroes instead of
empowering the real protagonists to become the heroes of
their own stories.

What do we do about it?

To begin with, we need to use terminology that does not
reinforce power structures. Conveniently, we use the term
"development," but this is not ideal. Binary terminology
such as "developed" vs. "developing," First and Third World,
North and South are divisive and imply positions of power.
While it is difficult to find appropriate words, we need to
think about more accurate terminology.

In addition, we need to be aware of colonialism and the balance of power that historically exists between us and the
communities we help. We are not there to tell them what
to do but to listen and learn if and how we can help. They
are not idiots; they know their situation better than we do.
Their needs may seem "bizarre" to us. We must give them
the confidence to spend the resources we make available to

them as they see fit for the good of their community. We must humble ourselves as respectful partners and actively ensure that local communities are and remain accountable to their organizations and projects. Local leadership and decision-making are requirements for sustainability where our work does not lead to dependency. Whatever work we do must be able to function in our absence. We are supportive, not leading.

Finally, before we begin a project, we must consider whether our entry into a community is necessary. What skills do we bring that are not present locally? Don't volunteer to build a school if there are local construction workers who can do the job. A better approach is to help a community with the resources and strategies that will allow them to hire local labor. In case our skills and presence (or those of any partner organization) would still be useful to a community, it is important to have a good exit strategy. How can the work continue locally, and how can we eventually make ourselves redundant?

SAIH Norway
Africa Corp. Radi-Aid 2.0
(A hilarious illustration of the white savior complex)
Video

HEALTHY ALTRUISM IN ACTION

One of the most important characteristics of busy people is that they will always be busy. Unless you make it a priority, it will probably never be the right time. The good news is that altruism doesn't have to take up a lot of time. Altruism comes in many forms, from shopping for your neighbor to donating to the Red Cross, volunteering at a home for the disabled, or donating a kidney to a stranger. How generous you are is a matter of choice, based on a set of circumstances, some within your control, some outside your control. Your choice.

Our parents used to say it all the time, and as children, we dismissed it as a myth. But even if we don't escape from it, time seems to fly faster and faster. Some invoke the habituation hypothesis for this, which states that over time we do more and more things on autopilot, storing fewer and fewer unique memories, and time seems to go faster. The others are proponents of the proportion theory: the perceived duration of a year depends on its length relative to your total lifetime. For an eight-year-old, a year is one-eighth of his life; for a forty-year-old, it is only one-fortieth. That's why those twelve months would last forever for a child and pass so quickly for an older person. All fodder for interesting discussions and research, but regardless of the theory, time flies, life is short, and we only live once, so we better not put off until tomorrow what we can do today.

We will never solve world problems, such as extreme poverty, by ourselves. Perhaps it will never be completely solved, even in the future. But we all can positively change the life of even one child. And that is certainly worthwhile.

Everything starts with attitude. Being kind and considerate in everyday life costs nothing and is the basis for "bigger" things. A few years back, we sold several soccer balls signed by Eden Hazard to benefit our projects in Peru. A lady was very interested and offered 50 euros, asking if she could pay it two weeks later, once she had received her paycheck. It turned out that, besides her job in a supermarket, she was also a volunteer in an animal shelter and wanted to buy the ball with her own money to cash it in during a raffle and thus help her beloved four-legged friends. Her story and her motivation were so touching that we were happy to donate a ball to her for free. Altruism in response to altruism. And it got even better when her story was picked up by some of her friends and acquaintances who started following and supporting our projects.

The choice

Before delving deeper into the various ways you can put altruism into practice, a few thoughts on choosing a charity. The choice is overwhelming; for example, in the United States alone, there are over a million charitable organizations. A few simple questions can help you with this.

- What is close to your heart? Goals that are aligned with your values and passions, possibly influenced by a personal experience, typically lead to a better and more lasting commitment. It is easier to (continue to) support a charity with which you have an emotional connection. In our case, this is children and poverty.

- What would you like to see change? Charity is like a way to correct something "wrong" you see in the world. That could be providing care to Ebola victims in West Africa or helping underprivileged children read at a local school.

- What organizations are doing this kind of work? Does their strategy seem clear and do you see any evidence of the impact of their projects? Can you find enough information to form a good picture of how they operate? Can you agree with their modus operandi?

- How effective is the organization? Do they solve problems or prevent worse ones? How do they work with the local population?

Here, we will focus mainly on how everyone can help to fight poverty, and extreme poverty in particular.

Raising awareness

Even if we have little or no financial or other resources, we can all show interest in a particular charity that is close to our hearts by reading about it, learning about it, and talking about it with others. You can show your support by sharing information with your friends and relatives. Word of mouth is the most effective and free way to generate interest and raise awareness. Every organization needs promoters, people who share messages via social media, for example. Before you know it, you'll be talking to someone who wants to donate or get involved. You'll be amazed at how small the world has become.

Making a donation

The first thing most people think of when donating to charity is money. Money is important to charitable organizations. It is used to help those in need and to pay for the operating expenses of the organization itself. Both large and small organizations have a role to play, provided they are well managed. Larger organizations can address larger issues but have higher overhead costs to fund their operations and fundraising activities. Smaller organizations can address smaller, more specific, or local problems, often more quickly, with much lower costs. Both are needed. The level of administrative and operational costs is certainly not the only measure of an organization's value. Smaller organizations like ours can often keep operating costs below 10% (or even 5%). For larger organizations, this is impossible as they need a structure to deal with (enormously) large problems. This is, of course, no excuse for incurring unnecessary or absurd costs or, in the worst case, abusing the trust of their donors. The "best" charities are not necessarily those with the lowest overhead and we, therefore, recommend looking not only at their cost structure but also at their realizations.

Donations can lead to tax advantages, which can have a positive influence on the amount someone is able and willing to donate. Countries such as Belgium, Canada, France, Germany, Italy, Switzerland, and the United States have a very generous tax approach to donations for official organizations.

Be realistic and stay within the limits of what you can afford. If possible, consider making a smaller, recurring donation rather than a onetime larger donation. You probably won't even notice it in your budget and it assures the organization of a more stable cash flow. Continue to monitor their progress, continue to learn about them, and continue to invest in them.

Before you make a financial donation directly to someone in need, consider the possible consequences. Let it be a well-thought-out decision, not purely dependent on the emotions of the moment. Can this distort the balance in a community? Why this person and not another? It is better to check beforehand with someone who knows the situation. Some cash donations have a very positive effect (especially if they are directed at groups or communities), others cause more problems than they solve.

Organizing a fundraiser

Organizations desperately need fundraising to survive in a world where structural support from the government is becoming more difficult. Some rely on professional fundraisers for this, others rely on technology and their networks.

Fundraising agencies use for-profit marketing techniques for nonprofit purposes. Applying an ultra-commercial system of numbers, goals, and money to a soft sector like charity feels strange, although there is nothing wrong with professionalizing the marketing approach of a charitable organization. Fundraising itself is not the problem, it is the way it is sometimes done and its lack of transparency. Mainly larger organizations rely on this type of fundraiser.

We prefer to use our own network. Social media today makes it very easy for anyone to create a private fundraiser for a good cause. A Facebook user can set up a fundraiser for his or her birthday in two clicks and, in no time at all, raise a nice amount within his or her own circle of friends. Donations are made on the platform and the total amount is then deposited, at no cost, directly into the organization's account. Easy for the fundraiser, easy for the donor, and easy for the charity.

If you prefer to keep it traditional, then organizing a yoga class for charity, selling homemade jewelry, a charity barbecue, a flea market sale or a waffle bake are very valid alternatives. Many people are eager to help, especially if invited to do so by their friends and relatives. It takes courage, creativity, and energy, but you can make a difference.

Never forget that some people have to live on less than two dollars a day!

Volunteering

We have so much more to offer the world than financial resources. We may have time, talents, and experiences that can be at least as useful. Many organizations need volunteers as much as they need money. Volunteering can be done on an ad hoc or regular basis. It is essential to make good agreements and clarify mutual expectations in advance.

Many people dream of volunteering in the field, as close as possible to where the need is. However, the reality in an environment of extreme poverty is much less romantic than what most people think. It's not a vacation getaway where you just get back on the bus when you've had enough. First, you don't go unaccompanied. You are not welcome there until proven otherwise. People suspect outsiders they don't know, especially in areas where child kidnappings are still a reality. Also, there are places where prying eyes are not tolerated, and keeping your distance is the message. We always go by invitation and announce all our trips and movements.

Be well prepared, both culturally and psychologically. Neighborhoods, where children live in extreme poverty, are not a pretty sight and are quite confronting for someone who is not used to this. It is important to manage your empathy and stay positive under all circumstances. Respect and humility are keywords. You are not the savior who has the answer to all problems. Adopt a humble attitude, listen and learn more about their situation and the circumstances in which they live. It is very tempting to pass judgment when something is not going according to the standards of your own culture. Without preparation, even with the very best of intentions, you will easily fall into this ethnocentrism trap.

On one of our visits to a community in the hills around Lima, we had struck up a conversation with one of the local leaders. We expressed our admiration for the way the mothers hopped over the rocks, seemingly with no effort, with their baby, wrapped in a colorful cloth, on their backs. Full of pride, she showed us how, in the blink of an eye, she folds the cloth in a way that the child is safely secured. The demonstration was filmed, with her approval, to show in a Belgian preschool classroom. When she heard this, she gave us the cloth as a gift with a big smile on her face. She added a few more words in her local dialect to Edwin, our guide, and said goodbye. A few moments later, Edwin took us aside and told us that this was the cloth in which she had been carried by her mother and in which she had also carried her three children. Our spontaneous reaction was to return this family heirloom immediately, which, according to Edwin, was not a good idea. After all, returning the cloth was tantamount to rejecting a gift and would reinforce her sense of inferiority. A much better idea was to accept the gift, take good care of it, display it in the classroom, and bring it back on a future trip along with a drawing from the children.

Besides volunteers in the field, organizations can often use people who can help them with several other activities, such as administrative work, events, or manning a booth at a trade show. Many of these opportunities require little or no training or experience. In addition, specific expertise that you have can also be very helpful. For example, a graphic designer can help with the design of an app, a marketing specialist with the development of a communication campaign, a legal advisor with the drafting of a privacy statement, and so on. These forms of help are invaluable.

Setting up a charity campaign

Altruism can also take the form of setting up a charitable campaign, where financial donations, fundraising, and volunteering are combined to achieve a specific goal within a predetermined time frame. Before you get started, remember to coordinate with the organization you wish to support. In the first place to understand their needs and way of working, but also to get their approval on the use of their name, logo, and other materials. Rogue individuals sometimes try to take advantage of an organization's name and reputation to extort money from good Samaritans, a situation that puts the entire charitable sector in a terrible light and should be avoided at all costs.

Several years ago, one of us, along with his then 14-year-old son, climbed Mount Kilimanjaro, the roof of Africa. The volcano is in Tanzania, a country where large parts of the population still live in extreme poverty. We realized we were privileged to take part in such an expedition and paired our trip with a charity event. After doing some homework, we ended up finding Amani Kids, an organization that has been working for years to take care of street children in Moshi, at the foot of Mount Kilimanjaro. Because of the instability of the local electricity network, the purchase of a power generator was one of their key priorities. We made some arrangements and during the preparation for our expedition we organized several actions to raise the funds and collect toys. The climb was a fantastic experience and the visit to the orphanage afterward was even more instructive.

A group of Scandinavians made a tour of South America by bus during the Christmas period of 2018. The trip took them from Rio de Janeiro in Brazil, through Argentina, Chile, and Bolivia to Lima, the capital of Peru. A few months earlier, a participant contacted us to ask if they could do something for the poorest children. Instead of spending a day in the historic center of Lima, they wanted to make themselves useful in the slums. After consulting with several local leaders, we could organize a Christmas gathering with a delicious meal for the entire community, financed by our Scandinavian friends and prepared by the local chefs. The meeting had an unexpected sequel when the group set up an additional fundraiser to build a kitchen in the community they had visited.

In 2019, 11-year-old magician Noah traveled around the world with his parents, making stops in places like Burkina Faso, Brazil, Peru, India, and Thailand. Everywhere he went, he met with the poorest children and offered them a magical moment of entertainment. By combining their adventure with a fundraising effort—they financed their trip entirely themselves—the family not only brought smiles to many faces but also gave a check of 1,000 euros to ten local associations supporting children living in deep or extreme poverty.

Amongst many others, these are examples of actions to "give back" to local people in need. Are you going on vacation to a region where there is poverty? Then check out how you can help. Do your homework, contact one or more organizations that seem interesting, or think about ways you can contribute positively. Not as a rich tourist or a wild benefactor who wants to buy off his guilt or win admiration by making a generous gesture, but as a human being who truly cares about the welfare of others.

Starting a charity organization

Finally, altruism can translate into the creation of an organization that seeks to make a long-term commitment to the less fortunate. This is a noble goal that requires thorough thought. Some charitable organizations start with grand ambitions and the best of intentions but gradually die out. The idea sounds simple, but its sustainable implementation in practice is much less so and takes time, tons of energy, and ditto passion. The following pages zoom in on several essential attention points, based on our own experiences and those of many others who came before us.

POINTS OF ATTENTION

Analyze your motivation

What do you care about the most? How important is this to you?

If you had a magic stick and you could solve one problem in the world, what would it be? The cause you are going to serve must be close to your heart and important enough to you so you don't get discouraged at the first obstacle. Understanding your motivation is the most important piece of the puzzle to ensure that you keep going when you feel like giving up.

Many charities need help. From animal welfare and environmental issues to helping children in poverty. It can be very specific or very broad. As long as it's important enough to you. You must be willing to make sacrifices and defend your cause in front of others who may have different priorities or opinions or even outright oppose what you want to do. Your inner flame must be strong enough, otherwise, there is a risk that it will extinguish quickly.

Think about why you want to commit to this cause. Is it something that has been dormant for years, or rather an inspiration triggered by a recent experience or encounter? Does your commitment come from genuine altruism or is it rather driven by external factors that may be transient? Admiration and encouragement from people you appreciate can be a stimulus, but often only short-term.

Getting the engine running is relatively easy; keeping the engine running is the real challenge. It's not enough to think it would be nice to achieve something. It has to be something you are passionate about, something you are super excited about, something you really want. Something you're willing to go the extra mile for.

You are brimming with energy, your motivation and your enthusiasm know no limits. Let it sink in for a while. A few days and a few weeks later, are you still as motivated as ever?

Discover the actual reality

What is the real problem? What are causes and what are symptoms? What is common and what is exceptional? How bad is the situation? How big is the problem?

Learn as much as you can about the problem you want to (help to) address. Don't assume you know or understand the situation. What you see is usually just the tip of the iceberg, not necessarily representative of the part that is under the water. Get first-hand information, go see the situation for yourself, and talk to people who face reality every day.

Don't let your emotions guide you. They are important, but they can cloud the picture.

Is the problem structural or rather exceptional? Is your perception based on facts or on what some people tell you? Are they facts or rather their version of the facts? Could there be hidden agendas at play? Who has potential interests at stake?

Approach the situation with a fresh and open mind and beware of preconceived ideas. If the problem differs greatly from what you initially thought, it is best to find out as soon as possible. Because of your enthusiasm, you may pay attention only to elements that confirm your ideas and feelings. Do not ignore any signs that would show otherwise, but try to form as objective and complete a picture of reality as possible.

It is tempting to see only the young lady with the necklace, but do you also see the old lady? Your perception is not necessarily the only truth. To understand reality, you need different perspectives.

Question your added value

What can you do? What value will you add? What expertise, knowledge, and skills do you bring? Are you really needed?

A good starting point is to analyze what other organizations are already working in the area you wish to help. What are they doing and what are they up against? What solutions or approaches have already been tried, which worked and which did not? It may be a good idea in the first phase to work together or to volunteer for an established organization that can guide you and where you can learn more about the situation and approach of these seasoned players. The expertise and experience you gain will help you avoid some problems in the future.

If no organization seems to be active within a particular area, try to understand why this is the case. You may have discovered a neglected or new problem area, but perhaps action has already been taken here, without results. Or perhaps this very area is being avoided by experienced people or organizations because of certain circumstances that you cannot assess. You can only identify these types of potential pitfalls by seeking advice from people who are well versed in the field.

Charity work is not trial and error. By misjudging or making an incomplete assessment, you can at worst cause more problems than you solve. Your presence may cause other organizations to direct their efforts and assistance elsewhere, which can be a missed opportunity if you cannot provide the necessary help yourself. Failures or ineffective interventions can additionally tarnish not only your own reputation but also that of the sector, making future help more difficult.

The road to hell is paved with good intentions. To avoid getting into trouble, beware of overestimating your own added value. Do your homework, talk to experienced people, be realistic and limit yourself in the first place to relatively safe interventions and methods instead of unilaterally tackling a delicate problem. Don't get us wrong: you certainly don't have to strive for perfectionism to get started. Just combine your enthusiasm and altruistic energy with a good dose of caution, realism, and preparation. And be sure that you are the right person to tackle the problem.

Determine your organization

How will you structure your organization? How close can you be to the field? What partners do you need? Where can you seek advice? How will you secure sustainability?

You've done your homework and took the leap. Take it one step at a time. It's not speed that counts but sustainability. You need a dose of idealism and naivety, but there must be realism in return. Don't be blinded by all the best intentions in the world. Pessimism is unnecessary, but be prepared that some things will go wrong or slower than you expected. The people you work with may not quite share the same vision, ambition, or level of commitment, after all. Some commitments may turn out to be false promises. Start small, give yourself some time, don't let emotions get the better of you, and keep your goal in mind.

You are not the first person to want to start a charitable organization. Technological advances have made the world a very small place. Look for similar organizations in different parts of the world. Look for players of similar size in your own country. Include them in your network, understand what they do well, but also what they could do differently or better. What are their key challenges? Exchange ideas and, as with so many things, you will get what you give. Find networks of charities to join (such as the Fourth Pillar or the King Baudouin Foundation in Belgium). They are an invaluable source of information and provide training and advice where needed. See if you can partner with other organizations to fight the common enemy (in our case, extreme poverty).

Decisions you make in the beginning will have an impact not only on the operation but also on the credibility and sustainability of your initiative. Surround yourself with people who share your passion. Different opinions are good and even necessary, but for the overall vision, you need to agree. Talk to others. Find out the motivations behind the decisions they made. If they had to start over from scratch, would they do the same? Any advice they can give? Look not only at successful charities but also at the less successful ones. There is often more to learn from failures than successes, and there is no reason to make the same mistakes. Think about how you will avoid the organization being or remaining completely dependent on one or a few individuals.

It is also important to understand the legal and regulatory issues surrounding charitable organizations. Inform yourself about the different options and their advantages and disadvantages. Opportunities and risks. Costs and benefits. In Belgium, setting up a non-profit organization is often the most appropriate legal structure, but it comes with several administrative obligations. For small organizations, this is not so bad, but it is better to take it into account if you want to avoid problems. If you plan to work with volunteers, make sure you understand all the implications (such as possible expenses and insurance). Good preparation avoids unpleasant consequences.

Many countries, including Belgium, have passed legislation encouraging altruism and charity. Get informed and stay on top of it, as the situation can change. While true altruism is the main reason most people donate, the possibility of a tax deduction is often an additional (and sometimes a decisive) argument for donating or increasing their contribution. As a small, start-up organization, you won't qualify immediately for the first few years, but you may be able to join the King Baudouin Foundation, for example, to enjoy some of these benefits, anyway.

How close can you be to the work in the field, now and in the future? Will you be able to monitor the situation yourself, or will you need a pair of local eyes? Will you have to rely on or depend on others? What partners will you need and who can you work with? How will you know what is going on locally? These are essential questions, especially if the interventions of your organization will take place a few thousand kilometers from where you live and you cannot be on the spot all the time. Today's communication tools make monitoring a lot easier, but it is utopian to think that you will do everything yourself, even if you build a team around you. Finding a reliable partner is no simple task. Western organizations are easily seen as a cash cow with infinite resources and before you know it, you are inundated with local "friends" who want to help you. Some with noble, some with less noble intentions. Ideally, you'll have someone on the ground who knows the terrain and local culture sufficiently well and who can help you identify one or more reliable partners or partner organizations. Good agreements will avoid misunderstandings and are essential in building a trusting relationship.

Develop your strategic plan

What are the mission and vision of the organization? What are the short and long-term goals? How will you achieve them? What are the core values and guiding principles that will help you make tough decisions?

Like any business, your organization needs to create a strategic plan that answers several essential questions. At this stage, the head should take over for a while. There is a lot of help available (templates, examples, advice,...). We will limit ourselves here to an overview of the key elements.

The mission (brief description of what the organization stands for and why it does what it does) and the vision (where the organization wants to go) have as their main purpose to create clarity and get all noses in the same direction. These will form the basis for the organization's objectives, which are interim measuring points on the road to the vision. Once these points are clear, the strategy can be determined, how the organization will realize these objectives. It makes little sense to talk about HOW you want to achieve something without clarity and agreement on WHAT (your vision and goals) and WHY (your mission) you want to achieve this. Or, like Alice in Wonderland, who is lost in the woods and asks the Cheshire cat:

'Can you please tell me which way to go from here?'

—'That depends on where you want to go,' says the cat.

'I don't care, as long as I get out of here,' says Alice in a panic.

—'Then it doesn't matter which way you go either'

You will have to make some strategic choices based on an analysis of the problem you want to tackle and an assessment of how you think this situation will evolve. There is little point in installing solar panels if the electricity company has concrete plans to supply power to the region within a few months. How will you raise funds? Are subsidies realistic or is it better to focus on online donations through social media? Who are the other players in the field? What are their strengths and weaknesses and how can we possibly be complementary? The more thoroughly this exercise is done, the greater your organization's chances of success.

The strategic choices then form the basis for daily and operational management and must be translated into several practical plans, such as a financial plan, a marketing plan, a communication plan, a fundraising plan, and a personnel plan. Write down what you do and/or what you want to do. This way, you also indirectly realize what you don't want to do. This creates focus and ensures that you don't just say yes to everything. The world changes, the situation in the field changes, and donor needs change: developing and adjusting the strategy for the organization is, therefore, a continuous process.

It is important to establish some basic principles from the beginning that will guide later decisions and avoid unnecessary stress or discussions. Suppose you are going to work in a country or region where bribing is common and culturally acceptable. Is this something you would consider, even for small amounts? What if it would allow you to act more quickly or avoid certain problems? Do you pay salaries or work only with volunteers? Will you help communities or individuals? Or both? It is crucial to discuss this in advance and make clear agreements about it. Once you face one of these cases, the situation can quickly become very emotional. By falling back on agreed-upon basics, you can avoid some potentially very heated discussions. Clear agreements now make hard decisions a lot easier later. Make sure that everyone is aware of these principles and that everyone sticks to them. They can, of course, be reviewed and discussed, but never during a crisis. Emotions are not a good guide for this type of discussion.

Embrace technology

How can you leverage technology with maximum impact at minimum cost? What are the technology expectations of your supporters?

Until recently, setting up and running a charitable organization was a cumbersome, time-consuming, and costly process that required many volunteers to keep costs down. The technological revolution has changed that. Small organizations are shaking up the nonprofit landscape. Some of these organizations were born in the digital age and have adopted the "digital-first" approach when planning communications, fundraising, or even the delivery of their services. They don't have a lengthy decision-making process, they take full advantage of free or low-cost technology, they don't rely on a large group of volunteers, they are highly agile, and can easily keep operating costs low. They also often bring the donor or supporter a lot closer to the cause they are supporting. They force the larger organizations to adopt a "digital-first" mentality as well.

In the early 1980s, a monastic nun came by our school to talk about a poor tribe she worked with in the Brazilian jungle. She brought a few Polaroid photos and local artifacts to illustrate her story. The school organized a sponsored walk and she went back with the equivalent of 1,000 euros, a small fortune. A few years later, Sir Bob Geldof, through his Band Aid initiative, showed us images of dying children in Ethiopia. The only way to get more information was through news reports and newspapers. Today, the world looks completely different:

- In 2018, over 17 billion devices were connected to the Internet.

- In 2019, just over half of the world's population was online compared to 24% in 2009.

- Every day, there are about 3.5 billion searches on the Internet.

Consumer trends and donor expectations go hand in hand. The perfect example of this is "swiping to give". Swiping to pay has become a part of everyday life, resulting in people carrying less cash. This has led to an increasing number of organizations having to rethink their fundraising and adopt new technologies to optimize donation opportunities. Your supporters know that a charitable organization is not a technology giant. However, they will become frustrated if they can shop online and make purchases with two clicks on their phone, but then must go through 10 pages of your website to donate.

Technology offers countless opportunities to connect people who want to make some of their resources available to others (money, time, or skills) with people who need help or can distribute those resources where needed. For example, we have developed an app that allows people in Lima with two or three clicks to offer an item for donation or to sign up for a volunteer assignment in the slums. Such digital applications can be very interesting if they promote the cause, appeal to the intended group of supporters, and pass an objective cost-benefit analysis. If this is not the case, it is probably not a good idea.

With the pandemic, digital transformation has suddenly become an even bigger priority. Charities can no longer hold traditional fundraising events or meet with their supporters on the street. Organizations that were already on their way to reinventing themselves digitally have sped up the process. Those who were about to start jumped into action. Those who were still hesitating to go digital are struggling to survive or have since disappeared from the scene.

Manage your credibility

How will you gain the trust of potential donors? Why should they support your organization instead of another?

You are passionate, you have a good plan and your intentions are extremely noble. You know that, your loved ones probably know that as well, but that's usually where it stops. Starting your organization is a frustrating period and takes time. It's natural for most people to be rather wait-and-see. Who will guarantee them that your organization will still exist next year? How will they know if your organization can be trusted? Your perseverance will be tested. This is the time to tap into your network and communication skills.

You can divide your target group into three categories: people who know you well, people who know you somewhat, and people who do not know you at all. Trust is something you build gradually, but you can lose very quickly. Always be honest and transparent, even if certain things go wrong. Start with the first group, where there is (typically) no barrier to trust. These are usually family members, close friends, and some colleagues or former colleagues. Speak to them individually and explain clearly what you are doing and what your plans are. Ask them if you can count on their support and if you can keep them informed of the progress you are making. Financial support is welcome but is not the most important thing at this point. You are primarily looking for contacts, free publicity, and people who will talk positively about your initiative. People in this first group will help you build trust with people in the second group: people who somewhat know you. Communicate regularly, share the progress you are making, and thank them for the support you are getting. People like to be part of a success story. As your initiative shapes out more and more and is shared on social media, it will also be picked up by people who don't know you at all (the third group).

Crack the social media code. Make sure information is always up-to-date. See which groups might be relevant to your organization. Is there an expat community in the area where you operate? They probably have one or more Facebook groups you can easily join. Do you have volunteers on the ground who want to share their experiences? Their stories are many times more interesting than your messages. Look for people who share your passion and gradually build your network.

Are you a member of a service club or do you know people who are part of it? Speak to them about your initiatives. These clubs are very often looking for interesting projects to support. Contacting well-known or influential people is a double-edged sword. If you know them personally, then you can speak to them. However, keep in mind that many other organizations are pulling on the same sleeve, and the chance that they will want to help is relatively small, especially for an organization with limited credentials. Put yourself in their shoes. Why should they support you? What makes your request so special? Make sure you are ready, that your story is strong enough and that you can get it across in a few minutes. First impressions are often decisive, and you can only create these once. Do not take any rejection personally. It is not a value judgment about your organization or yourself.

Communicate, communicate, communicate

How, how often and what will you communicate about? How will you further awaken the interest and motivation of your donors?

Most people want to know what you and your organization are about before they consider buying into your story and start supporting you. Regular communication is, therefore, hugely important. Vary the content of your communications so that you are not just asking for money. Use social media, take care of your website, send an update on a campaign, and let the world know what steps you are taking. Speak to the press, but only if you are ready and can bring a story that is strong enough.

Many people agree it is best to donate to charities that have a significant impact, but facts and figures are less appealing than stories. Communications that emphasize the proven effectiveness of the charitable organization do not lead to more donations. When giving to charities, many people act from the heart, not the head. Your organization needs to show that it is managing donations like a good family man and be able to demonstrate where all that generosity is going, but your message needs to go beyond numbers and pie charts. For many people, donating is an emotional act, and they feel more drawn to personal stories than to numbers or big statements. Put a human face on facts and statistics and get to the heart of the matter. Share this with your donors so they can identify with your projects on a personal level.

People support your organization because they believe in your mission. They stay loyal to you because you prove you are worthy of their trust and commitment. Transparency and reliability are the keywords. When you say you are going to do something, keep your word. When donors feel that their contribution has a direct impact on improving a situation, they feel empowered. Share specific information about what their donations support. Providing details about what you accomplish with donations creates trust.

For many donors, giving to charities is very personal. People who give because they have witnessed firsthand the accomplishments through a site visit to a project are incredible advocates for your cause. Their testimony is golden. Ask if you can use it. The more people see their colleagues, friends, or relatives involved in a good cause, the more likely they will join you.

Show passion, resilience, and persistence

How do you handle setbacks and criticism?

Even though you want to get results and help people as quickly as possible, starting a nonprofit is more like a marathon than a sprint. Passion is an absolute necessity. It is your inner compass that guides all your decisions and actions. It fuels you with intrinsic strength and inexhaustible energy while giving you inner peace. It will guide you through the more difficult waters. The sea may be calm at the moment, but eventually there will be headwinds and storms. There will be times when you wonder why you started this kind of ambitious venture. A project does not go according to plan, the fundraising is slack, you spend another weekend on administrative hassle... Do not let the slightest thing knock you off course. Think of the children who go to school thanks to your tireless efforts, or of the mothers who take to the streets every day to collect metal or plastic waste so they can feed their children. Surround yourself with positive people who join you in pursuing the goal of improving the lives of others. The result will outweigh the effort by far. Use your expertise, strengths, interests, and passion and you will never experience your charity work as "work." When you do what you love, you can truly make a difference in the lives of others. Passion radiates to other people. The energy it releases is contagious.

Treat every situation as a learning moment: what went well, what could be better, and what will I do differently next time? This applies to both managing your organization and your projects on the ground. Be open to constructive criticism, it will make you better and stronger. Above all, listen to the people or communities you want to help. Be humble and assume that they know what they are doing. Difficult life circumstances are a better school than the best book in the "life skills" category. If something looks strange, be curious and don't jump to conclusions. For example, many (Western) people find it odd that houses in poorer regions never seem finished. Steel wires stick out of the walls like stalks of grain. Why don't they just cut those? A logical question for us, a silly one from their perspective. Many residents do not have bank accounts and keep any savings they may have at home. There is a high risk that these will be stolen, so they invest in bricks and gradually build their house. Then, of course, those steel wires come in handy.

Altruism can usually count on social approval, but it can also lead to forms of social disapproval. Your family, relatives, or friends may feel neglected or unappreciated. Your loved ones may react apathetically or even disapprovingly to something close to your heart. Some people in rather individualistic cultures, even fellow altruists, may look down on you as if there is something wrong with you, or will not appreciate it if you speak to them again about your projects. Others will think you are implicitly condemning them for not supporting you or will provoke you to make ethical judgments about certain sensitive situations. Prepare yourself for criticism; the best helmsmen stand on the shore. By doing something but not everything, or by making certain choices, you expose yourself to accusations of hypocrisy. These are all human reactions that you must learn to deal with. You cannot please everyone and everyone is entitled to an opinion. Choose for yourself what weight you want to give to which reactions. Reacting aggressively to non-altruists or people who don't want to support you is not the same as being truly altruistic. You cannot and should not force people to be altruistic. Just as robbing the rich does not encourage charity and beating bullies does not instill kindness.

Take care of balance

No matter how big your motivation and altruistic heart are, you are a social being surrounded by other social beings. How do your partner, family, relatives, or friends view your initiative? There will be times when things get a little more difficult, where the existing balance at home or with your friends comes under pressure. Will you be able to fall back on their unconditional support at those moments? Will they encourage or discourage you? Give you a helping hand or tighten the belt? How does the setup of a charitable organization fit with any longer-term personal plans? These are extremely important questions that are best discussed at length in advance. No one has a crystal ball and can predict the future accurately, but it is best to make sure you have all the cards in hand to write a success story.

Investing in the creation and management of a charitable organization brings stress and can create tensions both within yourself and between yourself and those around you. Some altruists choose or change their careers to pursue greater positive impact, sometimes at a significant additional cost to themselves, for example by taking a job with more stress, lower pay, or further away from family and friends. Altruistic projects can also consume a significant portion of your evenings, weekends, and vacations, which can put pressure on your hobbies, your social life, or your family life.

It is important not to let healthy altruism turn into unhealthy or even pathological altruism. It can help to distinguish between your "altruistic" values and your "personal" values to balance the two and avoid potential conflict situations. Examples of personal values that influence our behavior include family, health, art, authenticity, and even certain forms of charity that we know have little impact but are close to our hearts. Choosing to do things that are more in line with your "altruistic" values than with your "personal" values might be considered a sacrifice that cuts deep. But perhaps "sacrifice" is the wrong way to think about such choices. Regardless of the ultimate choices you have to make when these values conflict, the stress that such tensions can cause should not be underestimated.

You founded an organization because you took the courageous step of facing the world's problems and admitting that you should do something. You have overcome your excuses. Now you may see no reasons you should stop helping and you want to do more and more, to work harder and harder, putting pressure on the fragile balance once again. Our contribution is at most a drop in the ocean, and the more we commit, the more we realize how big the ocean is. It is critically important to accept that you cannot and will not solve all problems without feeling guilty. Ask yourself regularly, "What if that drop was for my son or daughter?"

Finally, don't let unnecessary perfectionism guide you. Or in the words of Ingegerd Rooth, "*In extreme poverty, do nothing perfectly. If you do, you steal resources from where they could be better used.*" Distinguish between what is really and what is less critical. Unless it's for people's safety, 80% is good enough in most cases. Striving for perfection will only cause you more pressure, more frustration, and more stress.

OUR
RESPONSIBILITY

Most of us have reached a level of prosperity where our happiness no longer rises proportionally to the growth of our material possessions. Prosperity contributes to our happiness, but not infinitely. However, we can further increase our well-being by sharing our wealth with others. It makes us feel good, and there is nothing wrong with that: both our happiness and that of people in extremely vulnerable situations benefit. Everybody wins.

Having the opportunity and the power to improve the lives of others is a privilege for many people, one that comes with a sense of obligation. Taking on this responsibility is a great way to reinforce our personal values and be true to our own ethical beliefs. Our contribution to this world will not be measured by the size of our savings account, but by how we choose to live - and how we enable others to live theirs.

Our time on earth is limited. We all know this, but we usually prefer ignoring this. We get caught in the trap of believing that the future is infinite and that there will always be a tomorrow, although that is not the case. There will always be good and not-so-good reasons to not, or not yet, take action. Too many people have no purpose at all in their lives. They just float around, wasting their time, and before they know it, it's over.

At the end of your life, when you look back on the moments, the days, the weeks, and the years, will you be frustrated by the opportunities you missed or proud of those you seized? When we leave this globe, we want to be able to say, "Hell, we lived. And we had an impact. We did our part. We tried. We made things better. We made a difference. We led by example. Our passage was meaningful."

It's not about us, it's about all of us. It's about contributing to the bigger picture. You don't have to be a superhero or see things big for that. You don't have to sacrifice your existence or drastically change your life for it. It doesn't require you to eat one less sandwich. Turning your altruistic beliefs into actions, no matter how small, can make a difference. And if by doing so you change the world of even one person, you, for that one person, are changing THE world.

"The purpose in life is to live with a purpose."

—Robert Byrne

ACTION IN SUMMARY

- To transform our empathy into altruistic behavior, we must first correct our cognitive thinking errors.

- Without help, it is almost impossible for a family to escape the poverty trap.

- Initiatives that focus on health and education strengthen the basic conditions needed to break the vicious cycle of extreme poverty.

- Altruism in most people is not driven only by the head or the heart, but by both.

- People living in extreme poverty know best what they need most. To help them, listening is more important than speaking.

- Healthy altruism can take many forms and is not limited to making a financial donation.

· Setting up a charitable organization must be deliberate and well thought out to have genuine chances of success.

· Everyone decides what responsibility they want to take on.

Conclusion

We live in a capitalistic world that needs healthy altruism more than ever. Capitalism should not be driven by greed; it should be competitive, but also fair. The vast majority of us agree with this premise. Healthy altruism is a control mechanism that makes our world less ruthless and more humane. With healthy altruism, there is less heartache, less suffering, more kindness, and more empathetic thoughts and actions. It is altruism that guides responsible thinking. Without altruism, we have no rudder and our moral compass goes haywire.

Imagine Charles Darwin waking up today, after hibernating for over 100 years. He might be amazed at the technological evolution we have experienced (airplanes, satellites, computers, iPads, selfies, surgical robots, and self-driving cars), but he would be especially perplexed by our new patterns of social isolation, our overemphasis on and coverage of reality stars and extremists, and our disconnection from nature. He would raise his eyebrows and not understand why, despite these technological advances, there were still children dying of starvation.

Our steroidal, hyperkinetic world urgently demands more healthy altruism. Even though it may not be within our power to rewrite the world's important chapters of poverty, hunger, and pain, we bear full responsibility for how we think, how we behave, how we set priorities, and how we care for those who need help.

Let us bring out the best in ourselves. Let us take action.

"I never worry about action, but only about inaction."

—Winston Churchill

Case study - Children of Lima

THE APPEAL OF LIMA

Peru in a nutshell
Summary of key developments
Data

Peru is a country of great contrasts and clearly marked social differences. The contrasts between rich and poor are evident in Lima, the capital, which has grown from 5 million inhabitants in 1981 to 11 million in 2020. Most of the capital's population lives in shantytowns, known locally as pueblos jóvenes (young villages), most of which are on desert-like dunes near the coast or on the rocky foothills of the Andes. The transit traveler en route to Cuzco and Machu Picchu never gets to see this reality. The slums surround the center and the better neighborhoods. Their growth was mostly informal, migrants invading a piece of land, occupying it, and over time gaining ownership. More than half of

Lima was created this way. Informal settlements grew into formal cities, hovels developed into houses.

The gap is clear in access to basic services. While wealthy neighborhoods have had potable water, garbage collection, paved roads, and electricity for decades, these services are new or non-existent in the slums. Only in the 1990s did most of Lima receive electricity, and tanker trucks are still distributing water in many areas. Water quality is often substandard and the cost of getting it to the hilltops via dangerous dirt roads is 7 to 10 times higher than the cost of tap water in the city.

Lima's tremendous growth can be attributed almost entirely to successive migrations. During the second half of the 20th century, a massive internal migration occurred from the Andes to the capital. Peruvian anthropologist Carlos Iván Degregori used the metaphor of the shift from the "Myth of the Inkarri" to the "Myth of Progress" to explain these initial migrations. Most Andean peasants were nostalgic descendants of the Incas, hoping for a return of the Inca. From the beginning of the 20th century, they increasingly gave up their indigenous knowledge and identity in favor of the promises of modernity. They changed their outlook from the past to the future and gradually exchanged their Quechua language for spoken and written Spanish. Education, trade, and paid work in the capital opened new horizons and triggered migration. By the 1980s, about half of Lima lived in informal settlements and communities established by migrants in search of work, respect, and integration.

During the 1980s and the first half of the 1990s, armed conflict between the government and the rebels of the Shining Path movement accelerated these migration processes. The violence was concentrated mainly in the Andean region and resulted in entire communities in the central and southern highlands leaving their home regions in search of safety. The war killed over 69,000 people and about 600,000 fled, most heading for Lima.

In recent years, the reasons for migration have changed dramatically. The great disparity between rural poverty and urban wealth has only increased the appeal of Lima. Young people are leaving their mountain villages in search of a better life, better educational opportunities, and better health facilities. They believe that the future will be an improvement, if not for themselves, then for their children.

Migration to the city puts enormous pressure on the already overburdened urban infrastructure—water pipes and sewers are not available to everyone. Newcomers are forced to move out to drainage valleys of rivers or the sandy rocky hills around the city, far away from all basic services. Many end up in very precarious or even dangerous situations, often even more dire than the situation they left behind in the mountains. All this leads to an increasing "urbanization of poverty", a displacement of poverty from the countryside to the city. In the slums, physical and social isolation are intertwined, and the poorest households often live on the highest hills, where there are not even roads or stairs.

Economic migration very often happens as an individual, not as a family. For example, one parent goes to work in the city, or a child is sent to family in the city (sometimes on his own initiative), sometimes for studies, sometimes to escape the situation in the countryside. Sometimes, family reunification follows. Very often, families remain separated. However, family ties remain strong. It is significant that the Quechua word for "poor", *waqcha*, literally translated, means an "orphan", or someone who lives without parents, relatives, or social networks. Many poor migrants consider their families to be their wealth and as soon as they can, they seek each other out.

Finally, on top of domestic economic migration from the mountains, over one million refugees have poured in from Venezuela since 2017 because of political unrest, socio-economic instability, and the ongoing humanitarian crisis. About 80 percent of them have settled in Lima and depend on informal working conditions and street jobs to make a living. Some have left behind their families, their communities, and their loved ones in their search for a better life. The pressure on the city is enormous.

THE TRIGGER

During a trip in April 2016, I (Bart) got stuck in Lima for a day. Instead of exploring the center of Lima, I thought it would be much more interesting to visit the slums surrounding the city. After a brief internet search, I ended up with Haku Tours, one of the few organizations that organize such small-scale excursions. Unfortunately, their tour was full that day and just as I was getting ready to head into the historic center, I got a call from Edwin, the manager of Haku Tours. He was going to the shantytowns that afternoon and if I wanted, I could join him.

Edwin was born and raised in Villa El Salvador, one of the older slums of Lima. His mother was a close friend of Maria Elena Moyano, a lady who tried to organize life in the slum as best she could through the establishment of various food programs. She resisted both the government, which she accused of corruption, and the Shining Path rebels, whom, after yet another attack, she called terrorists instead of revolutionaries. She did everything she could to keep them out of the poorest neighborhoods and paid for it with her life in 1992. She was executed in front of her husband and children, and her body was blown up with dynamite as a deterrent to other local leaders.

Edwin had set himself the goal of helping as many children and families from the slums as possible outgrow their hopeless situation. He had broken the cycle of poverty and had studied and served several years as a sailor on large cruise ships. With his hard-earned money, he then founded Haku Tours, a small tour operator in the heart of Lima. The language skills he had developed during his travels, his sociological studies, and his life experience in the slums allowed him to grow his start-up into a well-run, stable company that employs several guides, drivers, and administrative personnel. He was especially proud of his anthropological tours, where he introduced small groups of tourists to life in the poorest areas.

Edwin told me he was in regular contact with the leaders of several local communities to gauge the situation in their neighborhoods. He showed me a small school he helped to build, several wawawasis (children's nurseries) he had funded with the proceeds of his tours, and introduced me to Senora Tuanama, the local leader and driving force behind several projects for her community. Instead of a few hours, I spent a full afternoon and evening with them. Years of life wisdom nicely packed in a big present, summed up in half a day. When Edwin brought me back to my hotel that evening, it didn't feel like the end, but rather the beginning. Of what exactly, I did not know yet.

When I returned home, I spoke at length about my experiences in the slums and both my wife and our five children replied in unison that 'we could do something, we had to do something'. We contacted Edwin again to find out what the most important projects were in the pipeline and what budget they would require. He spoke to us about the need for an additional wawawasi and a large soup kitchen to provide the children of a dozen such wawawasis in the neighborhood with a daily hot meal. This would require about US$10,000. We did not know how, but we knew we were going to raise this amount.

The project went well on both sides. Through friends, family, colleagues, and former colleagues, our family raised enough money within a month and the construction work started. We suggested several times to send him extra money, but each time Edwin held off and replied that he still had enough money because some costs were lower than originally thought. Through WhatsApp, we could follow the works perfectly, from start to finish. The projects were a success, the members and leaders of the community were happy, Edwin was satisfied, and we had a good feeling about it. Everyone had won.

When my professional job moved to New York, I became more intensely involved in this kind of activity. I returned to Peru and spent a full week with Edwin in the poorest neighborhoods. I learned about Edwin's successes and setbacks, his dreams, and his frustrations. About the difference between my perception of the situation and the brutal reality of the terrain. About the opportunities and the dangers, both for the children, the families, and ourselves. After rationally weighing the pros and cons and extensive consultation with Edwin, we decided our family would establish a non-profit organization to engage in a structural and long-term way with the children and their families. The non-profit organization Children of Lima was born in November 2016 and officially registered at the Tribunal of Commerce in Belgium.

Children of Lima
Non-profit Organization
Website

THE EARLY DAYS

To work together in full transparency and to offer the guarantees to the people who were going to support us, Edwin also set up an official organization in Lima. Reciprocity NGO was a logical new chapter in a story he had been writing for 15 years and became our sister organization in Lima. He is on the ground. We are behind the scenes. I put in a sabbatical period and started working with my family on the gradual expansion of our organization. Once the administrative hassle was over, we developed our strategic plan. We would stay small, keep operating costs below 5%, and rely heavily on free technology to raise funds and build our network. Our projects would focus on safety, health, and education for the children in the poorest communities, where extreme poverty still prevails. Decisions about projects would always be made in consultation with Edwin and the leaders of the local community. The leaders determine the needs, Edwin analyzes the priorities, and we see how we can help. In this order.

Our children helped develop and build our website and social media and together we deciphered the code to use tools with a sometimes negative reputation in a positive way. We infiltrated several Facebook groups of expats in Lima and

Peruvians living abroad, told our story, and soon we had more than a thousand followers. The world suddenly became very small. For example, we put Edwin in touch with a lady who wanted to help him in Lima and turned out to be a distant neighbor of his. Through social media, we built a small network of volunteers in Lima. Every time Edwin and his organization needed people to lend a hand, he sent us a message. We posted this on several groups and the next morning there were volunteers ready to help. Quick, easy, and effective.

Our fundraising, in the beginning, relied mostly on our network. I was fortunate to have worked with many people from different countries and with many a friendship had developed over the years. When they heard and saw that we were going to commit ourselves structurally to underprivileged children, we received lots of positive reactions. Some contributed financially, others brought us into contact with people who could and wanted to help us. Our network grew, and we became less dependent on a few larger donors. After seven intense months of talking, writing, listening, lobbying, and trying, Children of Lima was stable enough for me to return to professional work.

Meanwhile, together with our friends at Reciprocity NGO, we had already funded several additional wawawasis in new settlements. These children's nurseries are an important cornerstone in organizing a community. The smallest children are safe and receive a daily meal while the older siblings go to school and the parents can go to work. They also provide work for a few ladies in the community.

During this period, we got to know Bruno, a Belgian who is remarried to a Peruvian. Bruno was living in Lima for some years, and had a lot of experience with similar projects in South Africa, through his organization Tomorrow4Isibani. Bruno had been following us for a while through social media, saw what we were doing, and suggested helping. The beginning of a beautiful friendship and an exciting collaboration.

AT CRUISING
ALTITUDE

Gradually, we expanded our fundraising activities. Together with Hilde, one of our supporters, we developed a ready-to-use educational suitcase with a fully elaborated learning program for children aged 5 to 10. With the help of objects, videos, and other didactic material, Flemish teachers can fully integrate this into their existing curriculum, thus making both the children and their parents aware of the problems in the slums. During our Fiesta Peruana, sympathizers come to enjoy a typical Peruvian meal, dance, and music. Lovers of sports memorabilia and artwork can bid online for items donated by sports personalities and artists. In the meantime, we continue to communicate continuously about the progress we are making.

We made good agreements regarding follow-up of projects, regular communication, and preparation of new long-term projects. The interest of the children, sustainability of the realizations, and mutual respect between all parties involved are central. We learn every day. About the internal organization and functioning of a community and the prominent role of women in this (most leaders are women).

About the fragile balance between communities, the problem of child abductions in the poorest neighborhoods, and the presence of mafia organizations. About the hopeless unwieldiness of the local bureaucracy, the widespread phenomenon of single mothers, the incredible resilience of the underprivileged, the hospitality of those who have nothing, and the glaring ignorance of those who have everything.

Without the local knowledge and contacts of Edwin and his team, we couldn't play any significant role. Even with the best of intentions, we would have created problems both within and between communities. For example, it is impossible to reach families living in extreme poverty without driving through other settlements. To ensure safe passage, it is necessary to maintain good relations with these communities as well, so that they know who we are and what we are doing. Occasionally, during such a drive-through, a local leader approaches us and asks if we can help a family in need. Also, to avoid all misunderstandings, Edwin systematically informs the local leaders of our movements. When we asked him why this was so sensitive, he replied young children were still disappearing regularly, disappearances often attributed to foreigners.

It is also important to know where you can and cannot go. In some neighborhoods, prying eyes are not appreciated. Entering is at your own risk and with no protection from any police patrol (they do not go there). Drug bosses don't like unexpected visitors. Other mafia-like organizations try to make money from our presence. When we were building a retention wall to avoid the collapse of a small school, on the very second day, some dubious men offered us protection, for a fee. These are known intimidation practices, obviously not conducive to a productive atmosphere at the work site. The school director had recognized one man and visited him the same evening, together with the leader of the community where the school was located. After an enlightening conversation, they promised to leave us alone.

Cooperating with local government authorities is not always easy either. For our school renovation project, we needed official approval from a representative of the Ministry of Education. Although it was a public school, the budget was many times insufficient to keep the school open safely. Two classrooms had already been closed because of the acute danger of collapse, and more and more parents were keeping their children at home, which most times meant the end of their school careers. Getting the signature has taken longer than the renovation work itself.

However, the smiles, warmth, kindness, and hospitality of the people we help outweigh the negative feelings brought on by these types of situations. They have little to nothing and yet want to share everything. They offer us a meal while they are hungry. To refuse a meal, even with the best of intentions, is tantamount to saying that they are unable to offer us a decent meal. Accepting and sharing a meal with the children is considered a noble and altruistic gesture. Their self-confidence and belief in their abilities are very low, and their self-esteem is dramatic. The idea that people on the other side of the world, who do not know them at all, show an interest in their situation and care about their well-being and that of their children gives them a boost and is one of the best gifts they can receive.

Many people in the richer neighborhoods of Lima refuse to face this situation. They accuse the poorest children of being troublemakers and accuse their parents of a lack of education and respect. They state that single mothers just had to stay with their husbands and are responsible for their own problems. While they are just usually victims of domestic violence, covert forms of slavery, and sometimes, severe abuse, and rape.

There is nothing romantic about poverty. Children do not choose to grow up in poverty, let alone extreme poverty. Parents want nothing more than to give their children a chance at a better future. Usually, they know what they need and have the necessary skills to make it happen. All they need is a little push to reverse the downward spiral in which they were born or landed and thus break the cycle of poverty. We are proud to help a growing number of them, with the support of our supporters. In recent years, we have furnished wawawasis, funded soup kitchens, built staircases, saved a school, distributed donations, sponsored studies, and brought hope to hundreds of children and their families.

THE COVID-19
DRAMA

The nationwide lockdown announced by President Viz-carra on March 15, 2020, completely shook our projects and plans. The poorest families found themselves with-out income overnight. A few weeks later, all reserves were exhausted and the greatest sanitary and social crisis in dec-ades began. Peru was one of the first countries in Latin America to take far-reaching measures against the spread of the virus. Yet the country has become one of the worst coronavirus hotspots in the world. Hospitals were over-whelmed and people fled the cities to return on foot to their home villages hundreds of miles away in the Andes mountains. The fight against COVID-19 quickly became an extremely complex issue. A response had to be found to a global pandemic in a country with an under-funded health system, an informal labor market, a vulnerable population 20% of whom live below the national poverty line, and a massive Venezuelan refugee crisis.

The borders were closed, a curfew imposed, and people could leave their homes only for essential errands. In reality, the population followed the first month of the quarantine fairly well, but large gatherings in the markets still occurred. Over 2 in 5 families in Peru do not have a refrigerator—in the slums, this rises to 4 in 5—and cannot stock up on food for several days. They replenish themselves from day to day, going mainly to the markets, one of the principal sources of infection. At the La Victoria fruit market in Lima, for example, at one point almost 90% of the vendors were infected with the virus. People bought, got infected, went home with the virus, and spread it to the whole family. That most of the poor were shacked up together in overcrowded houses only made the situation worse.

People that live in shanty towns mainly work in the informal economy, without decent contracts, job security, or social benefits. They are forced to take to the streets and public transport to sell their wares in the very crowded markets. Staying home to protect their health means zero income and dying of hunger. Less than three months after the start of the lockdown, about 30% of Peruvians had lost their jobs, leaving a large additional number of families in poverty and extreme poverty.

The government helped the poorest families survive with small checks, but inequality in the country turned what was well-intentioned into a catastrophe. Only 2 out of 5 Peruvian adults have a bank account, the poorest are excluded from the banking system. They had no choice but to go to the bank in person, where the tightly packed waiting lines were a breeding ground for the virus. In addition, support did not always get to the right places; several investigations were launched after reports that officials had pocketed money meant for food aid. Many people fell by the wayside because they did not have the papers to qualify. The aid programs did not reach many people who desperately needed this help. Some went door to door begging. Tens of thousands of unemployed Peruvians returned to their villages on foot, afraid of the virus in the overcrowded city.

The support measures did not apply to immigrants and refugees. Their situation became more and more precarious because of their limited access to public services and health care, their uncertain legal status, and the lack of a family network to fall back on. Whereas in the beginning, they could count on support from part of the population, the general feeling of solidarity with Venezuelans quickly turned to rejection, leaving them completely to their own devices. Many made the arduous journey back to Venezuela.

The COVID-19 pandemic also highlighted educational inequality. Schools remained closed throughout 2020 and the vast majority of 2021. Families who could not afford private tutors or a computer and internet no longer had access to quality education for their children. In Peru, about one in three households can use a computer; most of the population does not have access to the Internet. For the children in the slums, distance learning is virtually impossible. The Peruvian government provides school broadcasts on radio and television, but even then, some children have no or only partial access to education. Until schools can safely reopen, the poorest children will fall further and further behind their more affluent age-mates.

The crisis has exposed the fragility of Peru's economic progress. Two decades of economic growth have raised many incomes, but led to few stable jobs and investments in health care, resulting in a dramatic human toll and much of the population slipping back into deep poverty. In the dilemma between protecting the health or the economic well-being of citizens, Peruvians have sunk to the bottom in both cases. The results of the fight against poverty over the past 15 years are being wiped out in one fell swoop.

The reality in the slums is that people live outside, do not have refrigerators to keep food for several days, have to go to markets to buy groceries, do not have bank accounts, and shack up with many people in a small space. The poverty rate and the share of the informal economy are high there, and medical health care is woefully inadequate. These are ideal conditions for a virus to wreak havoc. Officially, the pandemic had killed just under 40,000 people by the end of 2020, but in the meantime, that number has been multiplied by five. Because of the lack of testing, most deaths in the slums were not attributed to the virus.

Every day during the crisis, our team faced additional requests and pleas to bring food to the poorest communities.
Many families were no longer guaranteed a daily meal, and
children and single mothers wandered in search of food.
We had to adjust our approach from long-term projects to
short-term emergency relief. Helping families get through
this period unscathed was suddenly our imperative.

Edwin and his team had received special permissions to
bring food to the poorest regions. This was done under
protection to avoid looting. The communities increasingly
organized their own "olla comuns", rudimentary field kitchens, which most times comprised a large cooking pot on
a few gathered boulders and gleaning wood. White flags
appeared everywhere, the symbol of hunger. Thanks to the
support of our donors, we could deliver food packages to
over 50 communities, or about 10,000 people, in about
five months. When cooking outdoors became more difficult

with the fog season in May, we expanded our help to include the construction of covered soup kitchens, an added incentive for communities to continue helping their most vulnerable members.

TODAY AND TOMORROW

At the time of this writing, the COVID crisis is far from over. Compliance with the strict measures seems more difficult than during the first period. There is also no concrete vaccination plan on the table yet and the poorest families will not be among the first. To the anger of the population, that honor fell secretly to the political elite and their closest relatives. Inequality in all its glory.

The consequences of this sanitary, economic and social crisis will continue to reverberate for a long time. Schools have been closed for almost two years and tourism has come to a complete halt. A third of the population is unemployed and more than half of Peru's population lives in poverty or is at risk of falling below the poverty line. Not a pretty outlook for a country that had only just outgrown its status as a developing country.

Peruvians in general, and Peruvians in the slums in particular, are survivors. They are very resilient and we are convinced that, once the situation improves, they will get back on their feet and get on with their lives. We are more concerned about the children and fear that they will emerge from this period seriously weakened, both physically and mentally. Without help, many of the poorest children cannot make the step back to school, which would only perpetuate the vicious cycle of poverty. We expect we will have to work hard on educational and psychological support to limit the damage, bring back hope and get the children back to school as soon as possible. Until this is possible again, we are trying to reach out to the poorest communities with the purchase of some laptops and an internet connection. Social organizations such as "Close the Gap" are invaluable here. They help bridge the digital divide by making high-quality second-hand IT equipment available to educational projects in developing countries. In this way, we try to prevent the bridges between child and school from being completely blown away. Every child that eventually finds their way back to school is a victory.

It is in this context that we brought the CosmoGolem to one of the poorest slums, a giant wooden, humanoid sculpture by Belgian artist Koen Vanmechelen. This four-meter-tall giant is a prominent symbol of hope and evolution, a wooden protector who brings help to children in need. Although he is always silent, this gentle giant empowers children by helping them find their own voice. He invites them to communicate and share their dreams.

The CosmoGolem draws attention to the rights of children, bridges different cultures, encourages cross-border communication, and gets people moving. The CosmoGolem was adopted in 2006 by the Belgian nominee for the Nobel Peace Prize, Sister Jeanne Devos, as part of her fight against child labor, child trafficking, child prostitution, and child soldiers in Bombay. He gives these abused and "forgotten" children an identity and a voice. Peter Adriaenssens, child psychiatrist and chair of the Center for Child Abuse in Leuven, also 'embraced' the image and uses it in his therapy.

Together with several teachers and psychologists, the CosmoGolem will help some of the most underprivileged children in the slums of Lima to overcome the trauma and scars left by the pandemic and to look forward. In addition, it also plays a distinguished role as a catalyst for a variety of projects that benefit the entire community. Just like the over 40 giants that live in countries such as India, Pakistan, Tanzania, Poland, Zimbabwe, Chile, Mexico, but also Belgium and the Netherlands, he will bring hope to children in need. Hope for a future without extreme poverty.

Close-the-gap.org
Website

Koen Vanmechelen
Cosmogolem.com
Website

Koen Vanmechelen
Koen Vanmechelen on his CosmoGolem Project
Video

The inauguration of the CosmoGolem in the Valle Ecologico community in Lima
Video

Case study - Tomorrow4Isibani

KHETANI AND WINTERTON

South Africa in a nutshell
Summary of key developments
Data

Khetani ("place of choice" in the Zulu language) is a township of around 10,000 inhabitants, part of the Winterton community. It is a rural area on the banks of the Touga River in the foothills of the Drakensberg Mountains in KwaZulu-Natal, the easternmost province of South Africa. There are several small stores and supermarkets sufficient for daily shopping; the nearest towns of Ladysmith and Estcourt are about fifty kilometers away.

Khetani is one of the most densely populated settlements in the region. Growth was mainly informal and poorly planned. A lot of basic infrastructures such as paved roads and sanitation are little developed or non-existent. The houses, one-room dwellings built of cement blocks and corrugated iron, are neatly arranged next to each other on small plots of land. Most families have access to water and electricity.

As in many regions of South Africa, unemployment is very high. Many adults are unskilled or undereducated and have no prospect of finding a job to support their families. The average family completely depends on government grants, comprising child benefits (about 20 euros per child per month), a pension of about 80 euros for people older than 60 years, and a disability allowance of also 80 euros for people with disabilities. Most times, a household has to get by on just one of these subsidies.

In addition, about 70% of the township is a carrier of, or somehow affected by, the HIV virus, which has led to the breakup of families. Many families are headed by grandparents or orphans whose parents have died of AIDS. In a society where traditional values and norms are increasingly fading, these children are particularly vulnerable. They often become victims of violence, rape, or other forms of abuse.

Because of the combination of high unemployment and the effects of AIDS, many families live in severe or sometimes extreme poverty.

THE SETUP AND OPERATION

In 2005 Tris Beckers, a Belgian lady, emigrated with her family to South Africa to run a tourist farm. Soon she was confronted with the problems and needs of the Zulu population and she couldn't turn her eyes away from the poverty she saw and live her life as if nothing was wrong. At the beginning of 2007, she started the project "Tomorrow" which was mainly aimed at raising awareness about HIV on neighboring farms and among local families. The primary aim was to coach people to find help. In 2008, her good friend Sofi formalized her personal "Isibani" project (which means "bring the light" in the Zulu language) and the two ladies joined forces. The Tomorrow4isibani project came to life.

A year later, I (Bruno) was on a vacation trip through Southern Africa with my then-wife and our two daughters, ages 11 and 13. In Swaziland (now Eswatini) we met a Flemish couple (Christel and Eric) who, during a warm evening conversation around the campfire, told us about this small organization in the Drakensberg Mountains, which was on our itinerary. A few days later, Tris welcomed us to her farm, and we visited Tomorrow4Isibani in the Khetani community near Winterton. The confrontation with the raw reality in the township was a slap in our Western face. We heard stories about poverty, hunger, lack of education, AIDS, rape, and drugs and still vividly remember the penetrating smell of poverty that rose from the small village with its humble huts. It was the moment I realized that most Westerners do not know what real poverty is.

Back home in wealthy Keerbergen, we took the bull by the horns, and in March 2010 we laid the foundation of the non-profit organization Tomorrow4Isibani. Our vision was to help children and young people create a better world for themselves by reaching out and helping to bridge the gap. No simple task in the post-apartheid culture where racial inequality was still a scourge.

From the beginning, it was clear that we could not change such a situation overnight, no matter how much we might want to. We developed a long-term, 15- to 25-year strategy and the "5 euros, why? Because!" initiative provided a recurring, monthly cash flow. Actors Sien Eggers and Peter Rouffaer became godmother and godfathers of the non-profit organization.

Sien Eggers and Peter Rouffaer
"5 euro, waarom? Daarom!"
Video

This was supplemented by some existing income and additional donations and we outlined a strategic plan to provide the Khetani community with better prospects for the future. A few years later, the King Baudouin Foundation was also on board and the non-profit organization was approved by the Belgian Ministry of Finance making donations tax-deductible.

The biggest donor for Tomorrow4Isibani came quite early: Antwerp Diner, an organization created by Marc De Punt, then General Manager of Hilton Antwerp. Marc wanted to do something about the HIV-AIDS issue and founded the non-profit organization Antwerp Diner, together with some local friends. Since then, the initiative has grown into a wonderful, large organization that organizes a huge event every year to benefit 3 organizations: Sensoa, the Flemish service and expertise center for sexual health and HIV, the Institute of Tropical Medicine that researches AIDS therapy and Tomorrow4Isibani. Antwerp Diner has grown into the ultimate event in Antwerp and both the city council, large companies, the local catering industry with all the top chefs and the hotel school, famous artists, and many other companies support this annual event that in 2022 will have its 20th edition.

Antwerp Diner
Facebook-page

Originally supporting only a childcare center, Tomorrow4Isibani soon became the main sponsor of Isiphephelo ("refuge"), the former Isibani. The non-profit organization focuses mainly on projects involving help to children and young people, the most vulnerable group. This is done in close cooperation with the government services with which we have built good working relations.

The project largely comprises 2 axes: "Isiphephelo Outreach" and "Isiphephelo Place of Safety". The Outreach is a community center in Khetani, known to the population as "Ekukhanyeni" ("in the light"). Parents, relatives, school authorities, or the police contact the Center for various social and health problems such as teenage pregnancy, rape, alcohol and drug abuse, AIDS, conflicts, school problems, racism, official papers, and so on. After a discussion, the person in need is referred to the appropriate agency. Winterton is a rural area and for many poor and uneducated people, it is difficult to find their way to the right official administration. The center connects the needs of the community with the appropriate public institutions and follows each case until a solution is found. In addition, the center also delivers a monthly food package to an average of 150 poor families in Khetani and surrounding farms. Through local schools, young people are made aware of the different social and health issues. Finally, via workshops, they help people to discover their talents, stand up for themselves, and learn to live independently. Sustainability and independence are always at the heart of this.

South Africa has a desperate shortage of shelters, orphanages, and suitable foster care. Since the center was confronted daily with orphans and neglected or abused children, the "Isiphephelo Place of Safety" opened its doors in 2013. This is a safe, warm place, run by housemothers, where children are temporarily taken care of once they are officially removed from their problematic situation. They receive physical and psychological support and are integrated back into the school system. A social assistant takes care of the follow-up of each judicial file. The children can stay in the center until a suitable solution is found.

Tomorrow4Isibani
Non-profit Organization
Website

THE AIDS
PROBLEM

As indicated earlier, AIDS is a major issue in South Africa and particularly in the poorest communities. It is the primary cause of the decline in life expectancy at the turn of the century.

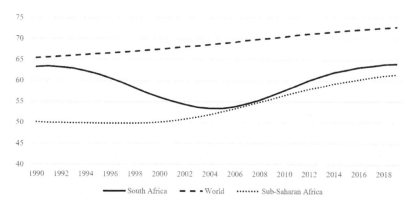

Figure 24: Evolution of life expectancy at birth in South Africa (1990-2019)
(Source: chart based on data from UNDP, http://hdr.undp.org/en/indicators/69206)

The Khetani township is no exception. About 70 percent of its population is directly or indirectly affected by the HIV virus. Unemployed people find it difficult to afford a cab to the hospital about 20 kilometers from Winterton to get access to tests, counseling, and treatment. For those with jobs, it is hard to get time off at regular intervals. All this resulted in many people not being tested or treated, whilst it is critical that people are aware of their status as quickly as possible and, in case they are HIV positive, get treatment and continue taking their medication without interruption.

To address this situation, the center got permission from the Ministry of Health to set up a VCT (Voluntary Counselling and Testing) clinic on site. This offers local people the opportunity to be tested for the virus voluntarily and confidentially. The center has a team of volunteers who are trained to counsel the patients before, during, and after the test. Early detection has already saved hundreds of lives. HIV-positive patients are referred to a specialized clinic for their medical treatment. In addition, the center helps them come to terms with their condition and understand the implications of living with HIV, the importance of strict treatment, and the necessary lifestyle changes.

Once patients begin their therapy, they can choose where they wish to pick up their medications: at the hospital or at the center in Khetani. Every week, pharmacists from the clinic come to distribute anti-inflammatory drugs. The center's volunteers assist in this process by regularly visiting patients at home. They gather important information about the evolution of their health and continue to educate and advise them on how to improve their life situation. While walking around the community, they also identify any other problems and offer help and advice where needed. One of the biggest challenges is to ensure that people do not discontinue their treatment once they start feeling better.

Every effort is made to help people living with HIV to live as normal a life as possible and to contain the epidemic. During the last ten years, the organization has dramatically improved the living conditions of many families.

THE IMPACT OF
COVID-19

The first infection with the COVID-19 virus on African soil was confirmed in Egypt on February 14, 2020. People feared that the virus could quickly disrupt the continent's fragile health systems. Therefore, from the beginning, most African governments took drastic decisions to slow down the spread of the virus. The measures we all know by now —avoiding shaking hands, washing hands frequently, maintaining adequate social distance, and wearing face masks— were put in place quickly. Countries like Lesotho declared a state of emergency and closed all schools before a single case was reported.

Yet South Africa quickly became the epicenter of the COVID-19 epidemic in Africa. According to a report by the South African Medical Research Council, an additional 145,000 natural deaths were reported in the country between May 2020 and February 2021. That's almost three times more than the 50,000 deaths officially linked to corona. The researchers do not explain these large excess deaths in their report but estimate that COVID-19 caused between 85 and 95 percent of them. With such excess mortality rates, South Africa is one of the hardest-hit countries in the world, based on the number of deaths per 100,000 inhabitants.

Besides the heavy toll on human life, the pandemic has resulted in economic and social devastation. Low-income people working in the precarious informal economy were hit the hardest. During the first half of 2020 alone, 2.2 million people lost their jobs. This made access to food and healthcare for these people much more difficult, which had a detrimental impact on their health. The poorest populations bore a disproportionate burden of the measures taken to combat the pandemic.

Increased inequality

The COVID-19 epidemic compounded the enormous inequality in the country. The black population is by far the worst affected. They are more likely to work in occupations with higher exposure to the virus, such as cleaners or decontaminators of infected areas, and can rarely afford adequate protective clothing. In addition, they have limited access to a quality health care system that is highly segmented in South Africa. It consists of a high-performing private sector—mostly funded by expensive medical aid—and an overburdened public sector that caters to most of the poorer population (mostly Africans). In 2018, only about 10% of Africans were enrolled in a medical assistance program, compared to 73% of the white population. It is the same group that most often goes hungry. Although, according to the Constitution, all residents of South Africa have the right to sufficient food to live a dignified life, the state fails to meet this obligation. Not in normal times and even less during the COVID-19 epidemic. The gap between rich and poor is only widening.

Urban versus rural

Racial disparity aside, there is a world of difference between fighting an epidemic in urban and rural areas. Strategies that work in cities are not appropriate for rural areas. In a rural province like KwaZulu-Natal, distances between clinics are much greater, there are fewer health facilities, and administrative systems are often stratified. Basic rules such as regular hand washing and observing good personal hygiene to keep the virus at bay are an uphill task for people living in an area where tap water and clean running water are scarce. Communication with the population is much more difficult—health workers, for example, go from village to village and spread messages with a megaphone—, medical teams are not welcome everywhere and many people are reluctant to accept the proposed screening and testing. At the start of the crisis, many older people even hid because they thought the government was coming to inject them with the disease. As with the HIV approach, the cooperation of "indunas" (traditional leaders) was needed to overcome this mistrust and reach the most vulnerable population.

Aids, tuberculosis, and COVID-19

South Africa is a country with approximately 7.7 million people who are carriers of the HIV virus and about 301,000 people with active tuberculosis. People living with chronic illness and a weakened immune system are at higher risk of dying from COVID-19. This may be one explanation for the large excess mortality rate. One of the biggest challenges facing the medical sector, therefore, was to protect people with HIV and tuberculosis from the risk of COVID infection, while maintaining vital health services for these vulnerable populations. The Outreach community center in Khetani played a very important role in this effort. As a trusted and easily accessible drug collection point in the township, it ensured that many at-risk patients did not have to mix with people coming to the hospital to be tested for a coronavirus infection.

Impact on youth

Finally, the daily lives and routines of the poorer youth were completely turned upside down when President Ramaphosa announced on March 23, 2020, that there would be a strict lockdown where people could only leave their homes to buy food or seek medical attention. All activities ceased, all businesses were closed, and everyone had to stay home. No more beers with the neighbors in the Ubuntu spirit of solidarity. Those who could not work from home were out of a job.

Most could no longer take care of themselves and without savings or income, life became very difficult. The demand for food parcels increased exponentially, including at the community center. Fortunately, we could count on support from surrounding farms to provide additional packages. The government grant of 350 Rand (about 20 euros) first came as a relief, but soon caused more stress for many young people. Some never received the grant. For others, the money from the grant was just enough to pay back the transportation costs to the post office to the relatives from whom they had borrowed the money. Still others had to wait in long lines only to be told that their application was not valid.

The pandemic and its related measures have not only caused great hardship for the poorest young people, but have also put their lives on hold. The full long-term impact will only become clear in the future.

TODAY AND TOMORROW

More than 10 years later, Tomorrow4Isibani is a stable organization with an active board of directors and a few dozen volunteers and social workers on the ground. The shelter is functioning properly and the various awareness programs are bearing fruit for the residents of the Khetani district: the AIDS situation is under control, drug use is quasi non-existent and children are attending school. Most important of all, the daily work is done by an autonomously running local organization with local people who know the situation perfectly. The pandemic makes things a bit more difficult and requires significant efforts from our staff, but we are hopeful that our organization and the communities we support will get through this period without major damage.

Until South Africa finds the key to reducing the great inequality that still grips the country to acceptable proportions, our help will remain necessary. If we don't help these children and their families today, who will and when? And what kind of message are we sending to our children and the next generations?

Answers to questions on page 14

1 – A (United States)

2 – C (Ethiopia)

3 – A (South Korea)

About The Authors

Bart Cools

Bart is a philanthropist, altruist, father, and husband who received an economic education in Antwerp and Louvain-la-Neuve. He quickly immersed himself in the various facets of Human Resources. After a career spanning 25 years in Belgium and abroad with various international companies, Bart took a sabbatical to rearrange his priorities. He used this period to set up, together with his wife Anne-Marie and their five children, the non-profit organization Children of Lima, through which they devote themselves to the children from the poorest slums of Lima, Peru. Bart lives and works in Belgium and guides organizations through various HR issues where the employee and the human being are central.

Bruno Rouffaer

Bruno lives and works from his home base of Lima, Peru, as an international coach/consultant. He is a labor sociologist, with extensive experience in organizational and cultural behavior. He is also known as a leadership rebel with over 30 years of global experience in leadership workshops and coaching. He is the author of "Self-Awareness in times of COVID-19 pandemic, a self-coaching guide to happiness" and the bestseller "NO WAY, The Big Bad Boss Era is Over". Bruno is also a popular speaker on Collaborative Leadership and Change and Resilience in Times of Crisis. He is a free-lance professor and co-founder and partner of Tomorrow4Isibani, Design & Art Laboratory, and Comunidad Peruana de Talento, among others. In 2014, he met Tulku Lobsang Rinpoche, an internationally highly regarded and respected Buddhist master, and together with Maaike Decock, he develops programs in Kathmandu (Nepal). Bruno is married to Fabiola Aranda Del Solar and is the father of Ella, Louise, and Camilo.

For lectures and more information, contact Bart and Bruno via www.everybody-wins.eu.

List Of Illustrations

Figure 1: Public perceptions of the evolution of extreme poverty

Figure 2: Comparison of global income distribution (1975 vs. 2018)

Figure 3: Different representations can lead to different conclusions (illustration)

Figure 4: The world divided into four income levels (2017)

Figure 5: The Dollar Street concept

Figure 6: National poverty lines vs. GDP per capita (2016)

Figure 7: Percentage of children living below the national poverty line (2016)

Figure 8: Proportion of population living below the international poverty line (2017)

Figure 9: Inequality in living conditions (2017)

Figure 10: Annual change in the number of extremely poor (2000-2020, in millions)

Figure 11: Countries with the largest likely increase in the number of people in extreme poverty due to COVID-19 (absolute numbers)

Figure 12: Estimate of long-term impact of COVID-19 on number of people in extreme poverty

Figure 13: Economic impact of the COVID-19 crisis vs. the 2009 financial crisis

Figure 14: Number of people in multidimensional poverty by continent (2018)

Figure 15: Dimensions and indicators of multidimensional poverty

Figure 16: Positive and Negative Experience indices - highest and lowest scores (2018)

Figure 17: Self-reported life satisfaction vs. GDP per capita (2017)

Figure 18: The cultural distance between the Netherlands and other countries

Figure 19: Top 10 countries in the CAF World Giving Index Ranking (2019)

Figure 20: Intrinsic versus extrinsic motivators for altruistic behavior

Figure 21: Evolution of life expectancy (1850-2015)

Figure 22: Evolution of infant mortality (1800-2016)

Figure 23: Overview of global literacy rates (2011)

Figure 24: Evolution of life expectancy at birth in South Africa (1990-2019)

Consulted Resources And Bibliography

Consulted resources

Aknin, L., Dunn, E., Helliwell, J. et al., (18/02/2013), "Pro-social Spending and Well-Being: Cross-Cultural Evidence for a Psychological Universal", Journal of Personality and Social Psychology, Vol. 104, No. 4, pp. 635–652, American Psychological Association, https://www.apa.org/pubs/journals/releases/psp-104-4-635.pdf

Allen, S., (05/2018), "The science of generosity", https://ggsc.berkeley.edu/images/uploads/GGSC-JTF_White_Paper-Generosity-FINAL.pdf

Bergland, C., (05/01/2020), "Is Altruism an Analgesic?", Psychology Today, consulted on 20/03/2021, https://www.psychologytoday.com/intl/blog/the-athletes-way/202001/is-altruism-analgesic

Borrero, S., Escobar A.B., Cortès A.M., and Maya, L.C., (03/2013), "Poor and distressed, but happy: situational and cultural moderators of the relationship between wealth and happiness", consulted on 15/02/2021, https://www.re-searchgate.net/publication/262501753_Poor_and_distressed_but_happy_situational_and_cultural_modera-tors_of_the_relationship_between_wealth_and_happiness

Brethel-Haurwitz, K, and Marsh A., (08/05/2017), "Why is it so hard to be altruistic?", Psychology Today, consulted on 20/03/2021, https://www.psychologytoday.com/us/blog/goodness-sake/201705/why-is-it-so-hard-be-altruistic

Chaffey, D., (03/09/2020), "Search engine marketing statistics 2020", consulted on 02/03/2021, https://www.smartinsights.com/search-engine-marketing/search-engine-statistics/

Charities Aid Foundation, "Five reasons to give to charity", consulted on 15/02/2021, https://www.cafonline.org/my-personal-giving/long-term-giving/resource-centre/five-reasons-to-give-to-charity#:~:text=In%20our%20research%2C%20Why%20we,their%20personal%20values%20and%20principles

Collett J., and Morrissey C., (10/2007) "The social psychology of generosity: the state of current interdisciplinary research", Department of Sociology, University of Notre Dame, https://generosityresearch.nd.edu/assets/11794/social_psychology_of_generosity.pdf

Countri, D., "Empathy and Barriers to Altruism", The Peace and Conflict Review, University for Peace, consulted on 22/02/2021, http://www.review.upeace.org/index.cfm?opcion=0&ejemplar=23&entrada=120

DeWall, C.N., and Baumeister, R.F., (2006), "Alone but feeling no pain", Journal of Personality and Social Psychology, 91, pp. 1–15, consulted on 13/03/2021, https://www.researchgate.net/publication/6952132_Alone_but_feeling_no_pain_Effects_of_social_exclusion_on_physical_pain_tolerance_and_pain_threshold_affective_forecasting_and_interpersonal_empathy

Dubner, S., (24/05/2017), "Are the Rich Really Less Generous Than the Poor?", Freakonomics, consulted on 22/01/2021, https://freakonomics.com/podcast/rich-less-generous-than-poor/

Farsides, T., (08/2007), "The psychology of altruism", The British Psychological Society, Vol.20 (pp.474-477), consulted on 10/02/2021, https://thepsychologist.bps.org.uk/volume-20/edition-8/psychology-altruism

Gershon, L., (29/06/2015), "Why Do People Support Charities?", consulted on 10/02/2021, https://daily.jstor.org/people-support-charities/

Hanson, R., (2007), "Giving Is Good: Generosity from Everyday, Buddhist, and Evolutionary Perspectives", consulted on 12/02/2021, https://www.rickhanson.net/giving-good-generosity-everyday-buddhist-evolutionary-perspectives/

Harbaugh, W.T., Mayr U., and Burghart D.R., (15/06/2007), "Neural responses to taxation and voluntary giving reveal motives for charitable donations", Science, 316(5831):1622-5. doi: 10.1126/science.1140738. PMID: 17569866, consulted on 10/03/2021, https://pubmed.ncbi.nlm.nih.gov/17569866/

Herrera, J., (09/2017), "Poverty and Economic Inequalities in Peru during the Boom in Growth: 2004-14", The Graduate Institute Geneva, pp. 138-173, consulted on 28/03/2021, https://doi.org/10.4000/poldev.2363

Index Mundi, "Peru – Income distribution", consulted on 28/03/2021, https://www.indexmundi.com/facts/peru/income-distribution

Index Mundi, "South Africa – Income distribution", consulted on 28/03/2021, https://www.indexmundi.com/facts/south-africa/income-distribution

Internet World Stats, consulted on 20/03/2021, https://www.internetworldstats.com/stats.htm,

Jules, R., (28/09/2018), "L'altruisme efficace ou quand philanthropie et capitalisme font œuvre commune", consulted on 05/03/2021, https://www.latribune.fr/opinions/tribunes/l-altruisme-efficace-ou-quand-philanthropie-et-capitalisme-font-oeuvre-commune-791825.html

Knafo, A., and Plomin, R., (2006), "Parental discipline, affection and children's prosocial behaviour: Genetic and environmental links", Journal of Personality and Social Psychology, 90, pp. 147–164, consulted on 08/03/2021, https://pubmed.ncbi.nlm.nih.gov/16448315/

Konrath, S., (02/2014), "The Power of Philanthropy and Volunteering", consulted on 02/04/2021, https://www.researchgate.net/publication/

291110268_The_Power_of_Philanthropy_and_Volunteering

Konrath, S., Fuhrel-Forbis, A. et al., (08/2011), "Motives for Volunteering Are Associated With Mortality Risk in Older Adults", Health Psychology, 31(1):87-96, consulted on 02/04/2021, https://www.researchgate.net/publication/51572746_Motives_for_Volunteering_Are_Associated_With_Mortality_Risk_in_Older_Adults

Konrath, S. and Handy F., (12/2017), "The Development and Validation of the Motives to Donate Scale", Nonprofit and Voluntary Sector Quarterly 47(2):089976401774489, consulted on 02/04/2021, https://www.researchgate.net/publication/321730372_The_Development_and_Validation_of_the_Motives_to_Donate_Scale

Kupferschmidt K., (11/07/2019), "Is the Western mind too WEIRD to study?", Science, consulted on 17/03/2021, https://www.sciencemag.org/news/2019/07/western-mind-too-weird-study

Lacetera, N., (02/2016), "Incentives for prosocial activities", IZA World of Labor 2016: 238 doi: 10.15185/izawol.238, consulted on 02/04/2021, https://wol.iza.org/articles/incentives-for-prosocial-activities

Lueth, K.L., (08/08/2018), "State of the IoT 2018: Number of IoT devices now at 7B – Market accelerating", consulted on 20/03/2021, https://iot-analytics.com/state-of-the-iot-update-q1-q2-2018-number-of-iot-devices-now-7b/

Macrotrends, "Peru Poverty Rate 1997-2021", consulted on 28/03/2021, https://www.macrotrends.net/countries/PER/peru/poverty-rate

Macrotrends, "South Africa Poverty Rate 1993-2021", consulted on 28/03/2021, https://www.macrotrends.net/countries/ZAF/south-africa/poverty-rate

Mateu, P., Vásquez, E., Zúñiga, J. et al., (15/02/2020), "Happiness and poverty in the very poor Peru: measurement improvements and a consistent relationship". Qual Quant 54, pp. 1075–1094, consulted on 28/03/2021, https://doi.org/10.1007/s11135-020-00974-y

Meade, A., (29/09/2014), "Emotive charity advertising – has the public had enough?", consulted on 18/03/2021, https://www.theguardian.com/voluntary-sector-network/2014/sep/29/poverty-porn-charity-adverts-emotional-fundraising

Muthukrishna, M., Bell, A.V., Henrich J. et al., (21/05/2020), "Beyond Western, Educated, Industrial, Rich, and Democratic (WEIRD) Psychology: Measuring and Mapping Scales of Cultural and Psychological Distance", consulted on 17/03/2021, https://doi.org/10.1177/0956797620916782

Ortiz-Espina, E., (2017), "Homelessness and poverty in rich countries", OurWorldInData.org, consulted on 22/02/2021, https://ourworldindata.org/homelessness-and-poverty-in-rich-countries

Ortiz-Ospina, E. and Roser, M., (2016), "Global Health", OurWorldInData.org, consulted on 22/02/2021, https://ourworldindata.org/health-meta

Ortiz-Ospina, E. and Roser, M., (2017), "Happiness and Life Satisfaction", OurWorldInData.org, consulted on 21/02/2021, https://ourworldindata.org/happiness-and-life-satisfaction

Park, S., Kahnt, T., Dogan, A. et al., (11/07/2017), "A neural link between generosity and happiness.", Nat Commun 8, 15964, consulted on 10/03/2021, https://doi.org/10.1038/ncomms15964

Peru Reports, "Poverty and Inequality", consulted on 28/03/2021, https://perureports.com/poverty-inequality/

Radovanovic, B., (03/2019), "Altruism in behavioural, motivational and evolutionary sense", Filozofija i Drustvo 30(1):pp. 122-134, consulted on 10/03/2021, https://www.researchgate.net/publication/331658840_Altruism_in_behavioural_motivational_and_evolutionary_sense

Rangi, N., (11/03/2018), "Les millennials et la philanthropie en héritage", consulted on 08/03/2021, http://www.influencia.net/fr/actualites/in,conversation,millennials-philanthropie-heritage,8216.html

Ravallion, M. (15/02/2016), "Are the world's poorest being left behind?", Journal of Economic Growth, consulted on 10/03/2021, https://link.springer.com/article/10.1007/s10887-016-9126-7

Reamer, F.., PhD, (03-04/2017), "Eye on Ethics: The Joys and Challenges of Altruism", Social Work Today, Vol. 17 No. 2 P.8, consulted on 18/03/2021, https://www.social-worktoday.com/archive/032117p08.shtml

Roberts, M., (06/11/2019), "The top 1% own 45% of all global personal wealth; 10% own 82%; the bottom 50% own less than 1%", consulted on 23/02/2021, https://www.cadtm.org/The-top-1-own-45-of-all-global-personal-wealth-10-own-82-the-bottom-50-own-less

Roser, M., (2016), "Human Rights", OurWorldInData.org, consulted on 08/03/2021, https://ourworldindata.org/human-rights

Roser, M. and Ortiz-Ospina, E., (2016), "Global Education", OurWorldInData.org, consulted on 07/02/2021, https://ourworldindata.org/global-education

Roser, M. and Ortiz-Ospina, E., (2019), "Global Extreme Poverty", OurWorldInData.org, consulted on 07/02/2021, https://ourworldindata.org/extreme-poverty

Roser, M. and Ortiz-Ospina, E., (2016), "Income Inequality", OurWorldInData.org, consulted on 07/02/2021, https://ourworldindata.org/income-inequality

Roser, M., Ritchie, H., and Dadonaite, B., (2019), "Child and Infant Mortality", OurWorldInData.org, consulted on 13/02/2021, https://ourworldindata.org/child-mortality

Sanders, M. and Tamma F., (23/05/2015), "The science behind why people give money to charity", consulted on

18/03/2021, https://www.theguardian.com/voluntary-sector-network/2015/mar/23/the-science-behind-why-people-give-money-to-charity

Scourfield, J., John, B., Martin, N., and McGuffin, P., (2004), "The development of prosocial behaviour in children and adolescents: A twin study", Journal of Child Psychology and Psychiatry, 45(5), pp. 927–935, consulted on 24/03/2021, https://doi.org/10.1111/j.1469-7610.2004.t01-1-00286.x

Sherman J., Ph.D., MPP, (28/08/2015), "What Most People Get Wrong About Generosity and Selfishness", Psychology Today, consulted on 23/02/2021, https://www.psychology-today.com/intl/blog/ambigamy/201508/what-most-people-get-wrong-about-generosity-and-selfishness

Siliezar J., (16/09/2020), "How the West became WEIRD", The Harvard Gazette, consulted on 17/03/2021, https://news.harvard.edu/gazette/story/2020/09/joseph-henrich-explores-weird-societies/

Smith, C., (27/05/2014), "What makes us generous?", University of Notre Dame, consulted on 08/02/2021, https://generosityresearch.nd.edu/news/what-makes-us-generous/

Smith, N., (2008), "Poverty, money, and happiness", University of New Hampshire, The University Dialogue, 41, consulted on 19/03/2021, https://scholars.unh.edu/cgi/viewcontent.cgi?article=1040&context=discovery_ud

Sokolowski, S.W., (09/1996), "Show me the way to the next worthy deed: towards a microstructural theory of volunteering and giving", Voluntas: International Journal of Voluntary and Nonprofit Organizations, Vol. 7, No. 3, pp. 259-278, consulted on 19/03/2021, http://www.jstor.org/stable/27927522

Stamos, A., Lange, F., and Dewitte, S., (06/05/2020), "Are poor people actually more generous?", Society for Personality and Social Psychology, consulted on 20/03/2021, https://spsp.org/news-center/blog/stamos-dewitte-poor-people-generosity

Tieffenbach, E., (03/2019), "La science du don", Université de Genève, consulted on 18/02/2021, https://www.unige.ch/philanthropie/files/3115/5292/2632/La_science_du_don.pdf

Vaccaro, A., (09/09/2015), "Point de vue: Les bonnes raisons d'être altruiste", Fondation de France, consulted on 18/02/2021, https://www.fondationdefrance.org/fr/point-de-vue-antoine-vaccaro

Vaughan, D., "What Is the Most Widely Practiced Religion in the World?", consulted on 19/03/2021, https://www.britannica.com/story/what-is-the-most-widely-practiced-religion-in-the-world

Warneken, F., (2013), "The development of altruistic behavior: helping in children and chimpanzees. Social Research 80 (2):431-442.", Harvard Library, consulted on 25/02/2021, http://nrs.harvard.edu/urn-3:HUL.Inst-Repos:12285465

Wilson, A., "Ubuntu: the African philosophy of giving", consulted on 17/02/2021, https://lessstuffmoremeaning.org/african-philosophy-of-giving/

Winnick, M., (16/06/2016), "Putting a finger on our phone obsession", consulted on 20/03/2021, https://blog.dscout.com/mobile-touches#6

World Bank, (07/10/2020), "COVID-19 to Add as Many as 150 Million Extreme Poor by 2021", Press Release, consulted on 21/02/2021, https://www.worldbank.org/en/news/press-release/2020/10/07/covid-19-to-add-as-many-as-150-million-extreme-poor-by-2021

World Bank, "Data – Peru", consulted on 28/03/2021, https://data.worldbank.org/country/PE

World Bank, "Data – South Africa", consulted on 28/03/2021, https://data.worldbank.org/country/south-africa

World Bank, "Poverty", consulted on 07/02/2021, https://www.worldbank.org/en/topic/poverty/overview

Yörük, B., (12/2014), "Does giving to charity lead to better health? Evidence from tax subsidies for charitable giving", Journal of Economic Psychology, Volume 45, pp. 71-83, ISSN 0167-4870, consulted on 23/03/2021, https://www.sciencedirect.com/science/article/pii/S0167487014000695

Bibliography

Collier, P., (2008), "The Bottom Billion: Why the Poorest Countries are Failing and What Can Be Done About It", Oxford University Press USA, Oxford

Ricard, M., (2014), "Plaidoyer pour l'altruisme", Pocket, Paris

Rosling H., Rosling O., and Rosling Rönnlund A., (2018), "Factfulness", Sceptre, London

Sachs, J., (2005), "The end of poverty", Penguin Books, London

Singer, P., (2015), "The Most Good You Can Do", Yale University Press, New Haven

9 782805 207211